GETTING PEOPLE TO READ

Volunteer Programs That Wor

GETTING

PEOPLE
TO READ

Carl B. Smith and Leo C. Fay

INTRODUCTION BY PETER S. JENNISON

*Sponsored by the National Book Committee
with the professional cooperation of
the International Reading Association*

DELACORTE PRESS / NEW YORK

Manufactured in the United States of America

First printing

Library of Congress Cataloging in Publication Data

Smith, Carl Bernard.
   Getting people to read.

   "Sponsored by the National Book Committee with
the professional cooperation of the International
Reading Association."
   Bibliography: p.
   1. Reading—Remedial teaching. 2. Illiteracy—
United States. 3. Books and reading—United States.
I. Fay, Leo Charles, 1930–   joint author.
II. Title.
LB1050.5.S486   428.4   73-7538

Contents

Foreword

THIS BOOK is the creation of many people. It is a good illustration of the team process, the pulling together of many contributions which brings a book to life.

In 1967, a challenge was issued to members of the National Book Committee at its annual meeting by John W. Gardner, then the U.S. Secretary of Health, Education and Welfare. The work of the Committee, a nonprofit society of citizens devoted to reading and library development, included the National Library Week Program and many other projects related to the social mission of books, and was well known to Mr. Gardner:

> I have followed the work of the Book Committee
> since it was founded and support its objectives with
> enthusiasm. I know how dedicated all of you are to
> education, to educational opportunity, to literacy, to the
> advancement and diffusion of knowledge. . . . For
> years I have been puzzled by what I regard as inadequate
> emphasis on reading, inadequate public and parental

interest in the teaching of reading. Reading is not just
another subject. It is *the* subject. If our schools fail in
that, all their other successes will not redeem them.

One of the difficulties today is that the problems
are so huge and complex that individual citizens don't
know where or how to get hold of them. . . . Citizen
action can become effective only when the global
problems are broken down into manageable and understandable parts. The teaching of reading to disadvantaged children is such a part. If we are to solve our
larger problems, this is a crucial piece of the puzzle.
Your Committee is well fitted to elevate this subject on
the national agenda. I hope you will give it some
thought.

We did. In January 1968, thirty members of the National
Book Committee and some invited colleagues met for two days
in Princeton to ponder possible action that the Committee
might take directly, or recommend to others, to improve
reading experience and opportunity; especially for poor, culturally isolated and/or minority group children and adults.
Among the eighteen points that evolved from the discussions
was this one: "Arrangements should be made for the preparation and publication of a book which would examine and
describe the innovative reading programs for children and
adults that are being carried on outside the usual school setting or in addition to it."

The group felt that the National Book Committee had a
responsibility to "publicize and make widely available the operational details of pilot reading promotion projects that spring
up in various places, since critical analysis and evaluation of
such projects can provide inspiration and help to other ex-
perimenters and perhaps prevent mistakes from being repeated."

Participants in the "Reading Retreat," as the Book Committee styled its "think out," observed that "a weakness in most pilot or experimental projects is their failure to include objective means of testing their effectiveness. They are usually started out of dissatisfaction with the way established institutions are doing the job, and they typically reach small numbers of persons. If worthwhile projects are to be continued, they must be incorporated into the institutional structure (schools and libraries in this case). On the other hand, institutionalization can reduce effectiveness. Experimental projects tend to attract the most creative personnel. Everyone associated with the project is eager for it to succeed, and the enthusiasm is infectious. For this reason, a whole series of 'pilot projects' may be more beneficial than any single massive institutionalized program. In any case, innovations are often a necessary prelude to internal reform."

An interesting sidelight shows how such ideas develop and spread their influence. The report issued as a result of the Book Committee's "Reading Retreat" was distributed to a small group of educational policy-makers which included James E. Allen, Jr., then New York State Commissioner of Education. According to his own testimony, the report contributed to reinforcing the convictions that led him in 1969, as U.S. Commissioner of Education, to espouse the Right to Read Program, the all-out effort to move "the skill and desire to read" to the top of the national education agenda.

The staff of the National Book Committee took its idea for the book, which would provide a survey, evaluation, and guidelines for volunteer programs, to its long-time colleagues and collaborators at the outstanding Department of Reading at Indiana University at Bloomington, Dr. Leo C. Fay and Dr. Carl B. Smith. They agreed to conduct a national field survey of existing programs and to help develop them into a book that could be a source of information and inspiration to others, if a publisher could be found. They confirmed the Book Committee's belief that there was nothing of this kind presently in the field, no one source for finding out what other people were doing, who was involved, how well the programs worked, and why.

There was only one problem: no money to conduct the field study. And so the National Book Committee approached Dell Publishing Company to see if they might be willing to publish such a book, as yet unwritten, in the public interest and on a nonprofit basis under Committee sponsorship. Their public-service minded president, Mrs. Helen Meyer, gave the project her enthusiastic support. The book would be published in a hard cover edition by Delacorte Press and in paperback under the Delta imprint. Further, and most generously, Dell would provide an advance sufficient to enable the research and writing of the book to be done. The National Book Committee, the nation's reading effort, and the public owe Mrs. Meyer and Dell Publishing Company a very warm vote of appreciation. Without their faith in the project, and their confidence in the Committee and the authors, this book could never have been researched or written.

The Indiana University Foundation accepted the funds for the reading department, and William Furlong, a young doctoral candidate who served as research assistant to Dr. Fay and Dr. Smith, spent the better part of a year analyzing more than 250 questionnaires, and conducting telephone and on-site interviews to get the facts and the flavor of many dozens of volunteer outreach reading programs. It was found that programs tended to fit into one of three categories:

(1) There were the supportive programs, which took place within the school, or school system, and were staffed, supported and administered, in the main, by the schools;

(2) There were the supplemental programs, which operated essentially from outside the schools, but in close cooperation with them; and

(3) There were the parallel programs—those which worked outside the school in all essential respects, and provided alternative programs for those who were no longer in contact with conventional schools.

Dr. Smith selected and organized the mass of material produced from the field study of existing programs, and drawing on his extensive knowledge of tutorial programs, parent involvement, and reading instruction, turned out a comprehensive survey and analysis of what it all seemed to mean. Then Peter S. Jennison, author and editor and a former Executive Director of the National Book Committee, did some excellent editing, putting all the pieces together in such a way that the book has become a useful tool for workers at every level. Finally, the detailed editing of copy and careful checking of facts was done by Virginia Barta of the National Book Committee Staff, and the manuscript turned over to the book's devoted and excellent editor at Dell, Catherine Cahill.

The manuscript was read by Dr. Ralph Staiger, Executive Director of the International Reading Association, and by other officers of the Association, many of whom made useful suggestions throughout the book's development, and in cooperation with whom the book is published. Some fifty other civic and professional organizations are helping to ensure that it gets into the hands of school volunteers, of college students and church groups, of senior citizens, and of all the other thousands of people who are at work throughout our country trying to make sure that children and young people and adults are making the most of their Right to Read.

January, 1973   VIRGINIA H. MATHEWS
                        Director of the National Book Committee

GETTING PEOPLE TO READ

Introduction

WE PRIDE ourselves, sometimes falsely, on America's being the biggest and best in so many fields that we do not really want to believe the facts about illiteracy, a disease which seriously handicaps millions of our fellow citizens.

The National Reading Center in Washington, D.C., created as an aid to the federal Right to Read program, tells us that America faces a reading crisis, a fact which is hard to accept but even harder to dispute when we realize that:

The 1970 Census reports 1,443,000 Americans cannot read and write *at all;*

One in 20 children is held back a grade each year, usually because of reading problems;

Eight million schoolchildren need special help in learning to read; teachers estimate that 43 percent of elementary-school children are in critical need of reading help;

There are at least 2.7 million high-school students who cannot keep up with their classmates because of reading difficulties, and almost half of all high-school students with reading difficulties receive no help in school;

In junior colleges, 30 to 50 percent of entering students require remedial help in reading;

At least 36 out of every 100 elementary-school children who need extra help with reading *do not receive it;*

If eight years of schooling is the standard for functional literacy, there are 19 million Americans who do not meet it; if the standard is twelve years, the figure becomes 70 million.

This dismal picture is even worse for minority groups in our culture; persons of Spanish origin have an illiteracy rate of more than twice that of the whole population; 85 percent of black students read less well than the average white student; and American Indian students in the twelfth grade typically have a 2½-grade reading deficit. Less than half read at the ninth-grade level.

If our sorry record of reading deficiency was confined to the educational sector, it would still be a matter of grave national concern. Carried over into the world of work, its economic consequences and cost, in personal and social terms, are staggering:

Five million job seekers are functionally illiterate;

One-third of all job holders are denied advancement because of reading deficiencies;

Over 20 million Americans age sixteen and over are unable to read, with understanding, at least 10 percent of the questions on standard application forms such as those for a driver's license, a personal bank loan, or Medicaid;

The functionally illiterate person earns an average of $4,000 per year less than the literate person;

It would require 15,000 new teachers and $100 million per year to provide reading help to children who need it in all the nation's elementary schools;

In 1970, the Bell System estimated that its companies spent $25 million just on basic education for its employees; and the subsidiary of another large national company claimed that the cost of training new workers to meet basic literacy requirements would be $3.8 million over a four-year period.

The vicious cycle of illiteracy, ignorance, and poverty is clear. We cannot afford to ignore this national disease, or to treat it with "benign neglect." Fortunately, more and more Americans are doing something to rectify this appalling aspect of contemporary life, by helping thousands of deprived children and adults to learn to read. The ability to read competently is not automatic, even though most of us take it for granted. For most of us it is a naturally acquired ability so central to all of our other pursuits as to be almost a sixth sense. So easily did we acquire the skill and habit that most of us cannot really remember how and when we learned to read. Nor can we imagine how alien and hostile the world seems to those who cannot read at even the survival level.

What does it mean to read? The authors of this book define it this way: the reader is able to pronounce words, understand their commonly accepted meaning and sequence, and interpret their message in the light of his experience. Divided into components, this definition means the learner makes use of several major reading skills. He needs recognition skills that enable him to pronounce the words. He needs to understand a series of words as a sensible message. "Take one giant step!" Does that make sense? The young reader may be able to picture the meaning of the word "giant," but the total meaning of the message may elude him unless childhood games have familiarized him with the phrase. Thus, personal experience, language background, and the way he has been taught to think all affect the reader's comprehension.

Because reading includes automatic responses (word-pronunciation skills), comprehending sequence (literal comprehension), and interpretation in light of experience (personal-development associations), many programs fit the definition of reading programs. Some concentrate only on a particular skill, while others seek to motivate the learner to recognize the value of reading, and indeed, to find the measure of self worth without which successful learning is an uphill struggle.

We are not suggesting here that amateurs step in where professionals have failed. School systems all over the country are giving renewed impetus to improvements in reading instruction, with some promising results. But few schools can afford the one-to-one tutoring which some children must have to master the skills and achieve reading comprehension. Nor can conventional institutions reach older dropouts, those alienated from the system, who so desperately need help.

"We are what we read" is a somewhat oversimplified, existential phrase, but the secret of becoming a successful reader—the key to lifelong learning—is an even simpler formula: skill plus motivation plus access. Once moved to acquire the ability to read wisely and widely—once "hooked on books"—a person's reading habits can be sustained only when books and related media are within easy reach, and if freedom of choice is made real and guaranteed. That is why schools and libraries need public support at every level, for millions of Americans still do not have access to them or to well-stocked bookstores; and why the freedom to read, assured by the First Amendment, must be constantly defended.

And so we find, in a church basement in Atlanta, three pairs of adults working on reading twice a week for two hours at a time. One person in each pair is a volunteer tutor, the other an adult illiterate. They are using materials provided by Literacy Action, Inc., an Atlanta volunteer group organized to provide reading help for adults. In Brooklyn dozens of teen-agers push carts out of the library and onto street corners. They hawk free books to the children and adults in the neighborhood. "Come on in," they say. "It's fun to read!" In South Bend, a woman visits the courtyards of a public-housing complex and tells parents and children that she conducts a free school for youngsters who have difficulty with reading.

In Detroit, 2,500 volunteers work with all ages, from pre-schoolers to adult-education classes in the public school system. In St. Louis, the number of volunteers involved in reading programs through the school system swelled from 25 in 1967 to 2,300 in 1969.

A concerned and competent layman can often provide what the school cannot. In a one-to-one or small-group setting, a volunteer works closely with the individual child and gives learning a personal touch, counteracting the dehumanizing influences of a crowded or regimented school. With this awareness and knowledge, housewives, insurance executives, high-school and college students, retired people and many others are coming together to work with professionally trained teachers, reading specialists, and librarians to help overcome the reading crisis. The value of their contribution—priceless in human terms—can be measured monetarily; using a $2.00-per-hour minimum, a thousand volunteers tutoring reading twice a week for a school year are giving services worth $160,000.

This book is about these people and the programs they serve, a record of what we call "outreach" reading programs, because they reach out to potential learners where they are. Some of the programs surveyed were located in the schools, but they were not part of the regular curriculum. Nor were they efforts to replace the school program, but rather to support, complement, or parallel it in various ways.

In interviews with more than a hundred people across the country, the authors were assured that there are increasing opportunities for reading help for the 26 million adult illiterates (of whom 80 percent are women) and for the children struggling with reading difficulties.

The engineering problem we face is to get those who need help together with those who wish to give it.

Volunteers perform most effectively when they are re-assured by the capability which comes with at least some training, and when they can work with a compatible age group. Some may feel a special affinity for very young children in day-care centers and nursery schools; others for elementary-grade youngsters; others for teen-agers; and still others for the physically handicapped or the elderly shut-in. Some may have experience that makes them good at reinforcing the acquisition of skills, while others are able to motivate reluctant non-readers.

The personal rewards inherent in volunteering to help in such a pivotal area of human development are deeply gratifying. But no one can deny that volunteers sometimes confront situations where frustration and red tape seem to conspire to discourage and defeat the most ardent helpers. A few years ago, for instance, my wife was tutoring a girl in the fourth grade of a middle-sized Connecticut city school. Donna had learned how to read fairly well, but was unable to comprehend textbooks well enough to keep up with her class. Making little headway with these, my wife went to the child's teacher to suggest that they might make a breakthrough with more interesting, unrequired books. "Oh," the teacher protested, "but Donna isn't supposed to be *interested* in what she's reading."

Such rigidity is, fortunately, giving way to more open learning in our public and independent schools; and where the emphasis is on learning to learn, reading flourishes.

This book is a step in that transformation. It is for all concerned people currently working in volunteer reading programs who want to learn of similar efforts. It is for those who wish to start programs in their own communities and need the experience of others on which to build. It is a handbook for the layman who is looking for an introduction to the techniques, skills, and activities one needs to help people learn to read and, as such, can be used to supplement other training materials in volunteer programs. We hope that the professional members of the reading team—the educators and the librarians—will gain a clearer understanding of the need for professional co-operation and of the importance of increasing their impact as professionals by enlisting the help of imaginative volunteers in innovative reading programs. Above all, we hope that the personal examples of the people who volunteer their help, the descriptions of programs at various age levels and in various communities, and the analyses of what makes some of these programs achieve happy results will inspire many more laymen to become involved in this vital team effort to help solve the critical reading problem.

If we fail, we condemn millions of the wordless—young and old—to half-lives of constant bafflement, bombarded from the media by signals and messages they cannot comprehend. The captives of deprivation, however, are not the only ones who need words and reading. We are a people on the move. We move farther, faster, and more often than ever before, which leads to a sense of rootlessness, of alienation from nature, from our fellow men, from the work of hand and mind, and, ultimately, alienation from self. Reading can help to restore a measure of self-realization.

We have to be able to read well not only to use the new and constantly advancing technology but also to understand the very nature of change itself. We have to be able to read well not only to get and keep a job in an increasingly special-ized, technological society and economy but also to under-stand the issues which animate and agitate that society. Beyond utilitarian self-interest as a motivating factor, there is a dimen-sion which touches the quick of American culture.

In *Walden*, Thoreau wrote: "Most men have learned to read to serve a paltry convenience, as they have learned to cipher in order to keep accounts and not be cheated in trade; but of reading as a noble intellectual exercise they know little or nothing; yet this only is reading, in a high sense, not that which lulls us a luxury and suffers the noble faculties to sleep the while, but what we have to stand on tiptoe to read and devote our most alert and wakeful hours to."

Tonight in Bombay one could see thousands of Indian students hunkering under street lamps, reading, because their homes have no light. Almost everywhere in the world, reading and books are more *prized* than they are in the United States. We are beginning to do something for the millions of our deprived children who are wordless and bookless; but many more millions, who do have access to words and books, are not being taught to read with a taste for the mind-stretching books Thoreau celebrated. Only a tiny fraction of our well-educated, affluent adults read in the spirit of Thoreau's "high sense" of intellectual commitment, probably because, as children, they were not taught to read critically, with a sense of involvement. Perhaps, too, the emphasis on rapid reading kills the desire for serious writing, leaving a mass audience chiefly for the condensed, the frivolous, and the sensational.

There is great promise, then, in these reading programs involving volunteers, for they can help the learning process, and add, moreover, a new dimension—a sixth, "high sense" of intellectual stimulation, purpose, and excitement for the infinite rewards of reading at its richest and fullest.

PETER S. JENNISON

1 ❧ One Person Counts

THE KAISER Sand and Gravel Company of Oakland, California, has a maxim painted on its bulk-cement trucks: "Find a need and fill it." The motto aptly applies to the volunteer activities and out-of-school reading programs which are described in this book. Volunteer groups, highly motivated individuals and public agencies receptive to needs of people, can serve society in many ways. Throughout this book we will stress two points basic to that maxim: first, people have been able to find needs; second, they use a variety of ways to fill the needs. The first task of the professional or of the volunteer is to make people aware of the real needs in their environment.

It is not enough for the individual to see social needs in a given community. He must awaken the community to an awareness of needs and a public commitment to solving the problem. Individuals can be just as effective as any organized body. Sometimes one curious person, seeing the world in a slightly different perspective, asks not "Why?" but "Why not?"

Dreams of individuals are converted into reality by hard

work, persuasion, overcoming frustration, and the mobilization of community resources. Mrs. Arthur E. Palmer had such a dream and made it a reality. Her "Buttercup" project is a success story. It is also a story that shows how one person, highly motivated, can make a difference—even in a city of ten million.

THE BUTTERCUP STORY *

In August, 1966, my husband and I were on a ferry bound for Swan Island, an island off the coast of Maine. It was a day of high winds and lashing rain, and the only other vehicle on the ferry was the State of Maine Bookmobile. It was a handsome, in fact luxurious, vehicle, although not very large, and was staffed by a driver and a librarian—both "Mainiacs," as they proudly described themselves, and both clearly very happy in their work. The trip to the island took almost forty-five minutes, in the course of which I had a chance to look around the bookmobile—glance at the books and talk to the staff. I remarked that perhaps not too many islanders would venture forth on such a day, but the librarian said with confidence that weather made little difference to her trade. "We can get here only once every two weeks, and they count on us," was how she put it.

Indeed, as we reached the wharf, a hundred or so people of every age were standing there, in wet-weather gear mainly, although there were a few summer folk who carried umbrellas and were having a struggle with the wind. We lingered a few moments to watch the operation and noted that the people there were returning books for friends as well as for themselves, and all greeted the staff with gratitude and enthusiasm.

We were much impressed and drove off discussing what we had seen. Yet in the back of my mind, I kept thinking of the children I had been helping in New York as a school volunteer. They were much further removed from the mainstream of American life than the children on Swan Island.

The Swan Island children were part of a community and knew it. The children on Amsterdam Avenue were not part of a community—they lived in fear and often had no idea whom to trust. The children on Swan Island were part of the world of nature. They knew trees, rocks, wildflowers, and birds and animals. The gulls and the seals and the fogs and the sunsets were all part of their lives, and at an early age many were already contributing to the family income by growing vegetables or as helpers on lobster boats, or at the very least, by clamming.

In New York I was encountering children of the same age who lived three blocks from rivers they had never seen or four blocks from Central Park, which they had heard of but didn't dare enter. I was helping children who had never seen a tree, had no idea of what a frog or a river or a hill was like and whose knowledge of animals was confined to cats, dogs, and rats, or a school trip to the zoo. Surely these children needed a bookmobile even more than did the children of Swan Island.

By coincidence, shortly after we returned to New York I had a call from a friend of my daughter's who worked for a foundation and who had patiently listened to me enthusing about the school volunteers. "We're looking for something in 'Poverty,'" she said, "for about $30,000. Have you got any ideas?"

I outlined my bookmobile idea, and she was most enthusiastic, so, urged on by the vision of $30,000 waiting in books and bookmobile for the children of Central Harlem, I made an appointment with the upper echelon of the New York Public Library. The lady who greeted me was very polite and also very able. She gently explained that $30,000 would barely buy a bookmobile and books, and would leave nothing for operating expenses.

I walked home in a belligerent mood and after conferring with my foundation friend once more, called Hertz truck rental. Mr. Sam Schwartz listened to my plea and said Hertz would be delighted to rent me a truck, converted by them to a bookmobile, for $5,000 a year on a two-year lease. Back to the Public Library and also to the library division of the Board of Education. Both groups said that, while they would never turn down a gift, they could not approve of my project, since they had so much better ones of their own. After all, I was not a professional, and consequently understood neither the needs of those to be served nor the facilities that (with enough money) could be made available.

While I was at the Board of Education I witnessed an incident that stiffened my back. A new school—a so-called "model school"—had just been opened in Queens. It contained many innovative ideas—classrooms in the round, movable walls to create flexibility in the sizes of groups, and so forth—and was consequently getting a great deal of newspaper coverage. The person with whom I was talking was obliged to excuse herself to answer an urgent phone call from *The New York Times.* When she came back, she apologized for the interruption and said indignantly to her subordinate, "Imagine! Anyone should know that it takes at least three years to acquisition a school library!" That school was being opened with fanfare as the model of what a school should be and yet it had no library! It was clear that she and I were not communicating; in fact, she dismissed me cheerfully, saying, "I know the New York Public Library will turn you down," and she was absolutely right.

At this point I was ready to call it quits and go back to my school work, but other school volunteers and several of the parents and staff with whom I had been working in Harlem said, "Look, we need this so. You can't give up so easily; please keep trying."

My husband secured me an introduction to the director of the Brooklyn Public Library, and I went and told him my story. To my joy, he said, "We'll back you to the hilt. There's a large public we want to reach, and we haven't been doing it. We are prepared to do anything we can to reach that public. It is important for the country to get people reading and educating themselves, and we can't expect an indifferent public to vote funds for the library."

This was the start of a happy association with the Brooklyn Public Library, which has been as helpful and flexible an organization as anyone who loves people and books could ever hope for.

With this backing and with the help of the library, my husband and I drew up a budget and wrote a prospectus for the project. In December, we learned that it had been approved, and in January we actually received the money.

The first step was to create a board of trustees and advisers, and I quite naturally turned to the people and organizations who had encouraged me to go ahead with the idea.

At the suggestion of the school volunteers and the Brooklyn Public Library, I had done some research which established that both District 16 and District 19 (East New York) were fertile areas for a project like mine. In both, the school volunteers and the library had community links which would help to ensure community acceptance. I put the choice to the Brooklyn trustees, and with some anguish they selected District 16.

District 16 is an area of great need which lies roughly two-thirds in Bedford-Stuyvesant and one-third in Bushwick. It borders on Brownsville. The population of Bedford-Stuyvesant is predominantly black. In Bushwick, in the section we served there is a minority of white people (mainly older) and a large concentration of Puerto Ricans, mainly non-English-speaking. We also discovered a large group of non-English-speaking Italians and were later to encounter many French- and Spanish-speaking refugees from the Caribbean area and also quite a sizable group (as it affected the schools in the area) of Romanian-speaking refugees from Yugoslavia.

Mrs. Louise Bolling, a longtime Bedford-Stuyvesant resident, chairman of the local school board, and a bookmobile trustee, joined our board. With her help and advice and with suggestions from the staff of the school district, I was able to lay out a tentative schedule and visit the schools, churches, and housing projects in our area. I was able, also, to speak to a meeting of the heads of all the parents' associations in the district, and we received publicity in the newsletters of the Bushwick Community Council, the Central Brooklyn Coordinating Council, and the Youth-In-Action newspaper. Unquestionably all this work was a help in getting us started and providing us right away with people who needed and wanted books. And yet, in an area such as this, communication is the most difficult problem of all. We learned not to be surprised at going into a storefront branch of the Community Council to tell workers of our services and to find that they were enthusiastic, though they had never heard of us in spite of our newsletter being posted on their bulletin board! We would find women sitting in front of one of our posters in a community center who were eager for our services, but had never noticed the poster. We would have children from across the street discover us only after two months of our presence at the same stop each week. Life in a ghetto area is such that in order to survive, an inhabitant learns to tune out a great many sights and sounds. It makes communication, except by word of mouth, very difficult.

For almost a month, with the help of my trustees, I interviewed prospective staff. I was looking for a man or woman from the community who could both drive the vehicle and administer the operation. I was looking for a part-time librarian to handle book selection with me and to supervise.

Eventually I was lucky enough to find an excellent librarian, Sarah Koerner, and an outstanding administrator, Lillian Butler, the wife of a minister in the area.

We made out a list of titles (based in large part on their exhaustive knowledge of children's literature and on school volunteer experience), and Mr. Evan Thomas undertook the enormous task of writing every publisher whose books were on my list and asking for a first set of books free to get the project under way.

Meanwhile, the Hertz Company and I were struggling with the details of turning an eighteen-foot panel truck into a warm, cozy, but unusual kind of bookmobile. It was a first for both of us, and we had many interesting experiences. I wanted to be quite sure a woman could drive such a truck comfortably, and managed to stall it in the middle of Tenth Avenue and Thirty-fourth Street in Manhattan, a moment neither the Hertz man nor I shall ever forget.

The Brooklyn Public Library generously gave me a corner of the basement of the Saratoga Reading Center, a branch of the library in Bushwick. The Chase Manhattan Bank waved a magic wand and turned the corner into an office lined with bookshelves and complete with wall-to-wall carpeting.

Suddenly, it was the middle of June. The publishers, led by Evan, had been most generous and either given or sold at a huge discount, from ten to twenty copies of each of my titles, and the books were pouring in. My tiny staff and I confronted the fact that we had roughly 10,000 books and 500 dry mounted prints to process in ten working days. Then we had to arrange and load the truck, which had not yet arrived. It was mysteriously always "almost ready," according to Hertz, and in the end did not appear till July 1.

We were having a grand and well-publicized opening of our service, with Mayor John Lindsay, George Champion, former president of the Chase Manhattan Bank, and other dignitaries and speakers; we just plain had to be ready.

It seemed impossible, but Mrs. Farmer and her block association wrought magic. A constant stream of black and white and old and young showed up at our door. Often they had no idea what they had come for or were expected to do but would say, "Audrey Farmer said I had to help, and here I am." It was an exciting experience to watch a small but well-knit community in action, and on July 3 we loaded the truck—now known (via Mrs. Farmer) as Buttercup (she was a lovely yellow)—with books and pictures, put gay posters on the outside and a warm red rug on the floor.

The grand opening came on July 5. None of us had any idea what to expect. The Chase had put posters around. Would anyone come? I, at least, did not yet understand how empty life was for most children on a summer day in a ghetto in Brooklyn. We were mobbed by a polite, confused, and appreciative group—many of whom confused the idea of books with the free Good Humors and quite genuinely (we later learned) thought that the books also were a free gift. With the help of a good many volunteers, we served over 300 people and gave out over 300 books, only about 100 of which we ever saw again.

July 5 was heady stuff; reporters, bands, and publicity. On July 6 we crept out on our appointed rounds and were happy to find that we met a warm response.

The truck itself was blatant and unusual enough so that many children, at least, who are more alive and less harried than adults, did notice us. One rear door was wide open, enabling a passerby to see the interior, and so was the front door. Over the front door was a sign of welcome in English and Spanish, and we were emblazoned with signs explaining that we were the Bushwick-Bedford-Stuyvesant Traveling Library.

Children, of course, were the first to clamber aboard, and since we were new, there was a considerable amount of confusion. Many of our clientele had never before encountered the library concept and were incredulous when we explained that the books were free. Some children returned each week for two or three weeks without registering before they would believe there wasn't a catch. Others had to get permission from the parents, and it came slowly. "My father says, don't never give your name and address to nobody," confided one little girl, and it took two weeks of eyeing *Curious George* before she gathered strength to make him understand that here it was worth taking a chance and registering. Many teen-agers came aboard and wanted to buy our books. "How can I tell where I'll be next week?" said one. "Here, sell me this [*Diamonds Are Forever*], and neither one of us will have to worry." We held our ground. We were a *library*, although we were willing to sell reference books—dictionaries, atlases, cookbooks, Dr. Spock, books on judo and karate.

That summer only the judo and karate books sold. But people borrowed books. We had a growing trade. In the first eighteen months people borrowed books and we had worked up to a circulation of over one thousand people a week.

Obviously, to take care of so many people we had had to add to our staff. We had an administrator, a clerk, a driver who was also a general factotum and a specialist in our art prints, and a new and enthusiastic Neighborhood Youth Corps boy. All either lived in the area or knew it well and had friends and relatives who lived there. The Youth Corps boy was a high-school dropout who liked reading and had ambitions. Our clerk and administrator had school-age children and cared deeply about helping children. Our driver had grown up in Bedford-Stuyvesant and had grandchildren in the area. The staff felt at home with the clientele, and vice versa.

The composition of the staff was one difference from the standard library operation. A second difference was the kind of material we carried—only 800 titles at any one time, but between ten and twenty of each title. The titles had been picked based on school volunteer experience and were intended to appeal to a wide age range but a low reading level. The books were arranged with the covers showing, as they are in stationery or paperback stores, and were arranged by category, with no segregation as to age groups. This meant that, for example, in the mystery section there was a hot integrated mystery on second-grade reading level near the floor, and the reading and interest level rose to the ceiling, where one could find Chester Himes, James Bond, and Sherlock Holmes. The advantage lay in the fact that a high-school dropout who was interested in sports could pick a fourth-grade book on football with no questions asked, a grandmother could borrow *Bible Stories* for children, and a twelve-year-old could take out *The Autobiography of Malcolm X*. Additionally, the fact that most of our books were paperbacks reassured our customers. Many of our most popular biographies (*Martin Luther King—Peaceful Warrior, Jackie Robinson*, etc.) had originally come out in hardcover format clearly intended for the juvenile market. In paperback form they were indistinguishable from books intended for the adult market, and yet the fact that they were on a fifth-grade reading level made them rewarding for people who were not accustomed to reading.

People of all ages invariably chose paperbacks over our few hardcover books. Perhaps unconsciously they related paperbacks to one of the few pleasant experiences they had had with the written word—comics. Even more important, the people who used Buttercup were often so beset economically that they were fearful. They asked us, "What if we borrow a book and Something Happens?" I use capitals deliberately, because that is how it seemed to them. Something over which they had little or no control Happened, and they were in trouble. If they were going to be in trouble, and they were sure they were, better to borrow a paperback.

A third difference was the fact that all the staff were asked to read our books and to be prepared to recommend titles to our clientele. Getting to know our stock and being able to recommend a book from personal experience of enjoyment made a great deal of difference and created an instant rapport with the people who came aboard that is entirely different from any I have ever seen in a library. Every customer was a potential friend, and the atmosphere was relaxed and easy except when we had a surge of customers all at once. Many lonely people came first for the friendliness and then later came to value the books. Many children came first for the sense of importance it gave them to be able to have a *choice* (something that they had perhaps rarely experienced) and to have an adult ask what they wanted and what they were interested in and whether they had enjoyed a book. It was fun and exciting to see a child at first so inarticulate he could barely stammer "sports" or "mysteries" or "I want a funny book" when first asked his choice, and six weeks later walk in boldly and greet the staff and comment on the book he was returning.

Another important factor in the success of Buttercup—and, I am sure, one of the main reasons for its high rate of return (90 percent of our books came back)—was the fact that we had a system whereby (although we had library cards for each customer) no one could ever lose his library card: we kept them all. We also had no fines for lateness. If a family catastrophe happened and a child was sent to live with relatives for a while, when he returned weeks later, he was given a warm welcome and no questions asked. As a result, people could afford to return books that were well overdue. However, we issued only one book to a customer. If people who were not very used to reading read a book a week, we felt (and so did they) that they had done well. If they were real readers—three or four books a week—they belonged in the public library.

Another bookmobile innovation was the fact that we

carried museum-quality prints—dry-mounted—which we lent
to adults. The purpose of this was not only to bring pleasure to
people in drab surroundings but also to encourage observation
on the part of the children and especially to encourage family
conversation. Too many children hear little at home from their
overburdened parents except commands such as, "Get up, get
to bed, quit that racket, etc." Such a child comes to school so
inarticulate that he cannot say a sentence, and of course, speaking and a vocabulary are the first key to reading. We carried a
viewer with thirty slides of our prints mounted on the back
wall of the truck. That way, a customer could point and say,
"I want Number 25," and one of the staff, usually Mr. Jones,
since he took special pride in the pictures, would fetch the
print from a container mounted over the wheel hub. We gave
the borrower a hanger (a heavy paper sticky on both sides)
that would support the print and in no way damage the wall it
was hung on—an important factor for those who lived in
projects. The picture idea was only modestly successful. Many
people were too fearful. All too often, I would hear a mother
say, "Oh, that's *too* beautiful. I'm afraid my children would
hurt it. Lady, if I saved a lot of money, isn't there any way I
could buy it off you?" I had had very little idea of what would
be popular and had tried to produce great variety and lots of
color. Our most popular prints were a magnificent Rubens
portrait of a black, an El Greco *Virgin and Angels,* and a
Botticelli *Virgin and Child.* Van Gogh's *Sunflowers* was the
best-liked still life, and a Dufy landscape of the Riviera (which
reminded the islanders of home, since it resembled a Caribbean
scene) was borrowed quite often. Later, I happened across
three prints by Tretchikoff. They were pictures of African
women—two of them quite dramatic, and all three very beautiful. These prints were so much liked that the borrowers refused to return them. One woman who conscientiously returned her and her children's books each week absolutely

refused to give up her picture, and we found that if we insisted on getting back these prints, all we did was lose a friend and customer. These prints, by a living artist, were very expensive ($9.50 dry-mounted), but the prints that were, so to speak, in the public domain were much cheaper ($1.00 apiece if bought in quantity), and I imagine that a store which carried such prints in an area like this could sell a great many at a fair profit. Although I do not feel my art venture worked out as I had planned, I learned from it, and it was clear that the interest in art and the love of art was intense. If a foundation could reproduce prints of Ezra Jack Keats' book illustrations and Tom Feeling's *Madonna and Child* (to give just two examples) at a reasonable price, people would flock to buy them, and it would affect the lives of many children. I have seen a withdrawn and apathetic child come alive when he saw the bright colors of *Snowy Day*. I have seen the excitement of a little girl when she realized Feeling's Madonna was "black—just like me!"

Selling reference books was another innovation that was only modestly successful. The problem was that the material which people needed didn't exist. We had quite a few young women come aboard (especially near our health-center stops) and say, "The doctor wants me to get a book on how to take care of the baby." I would produce Dr. Spock, and the mother would say, "Oh, yes, that's the name he said; I'll buy it." I would insist that she look it over for a while before I took her money, and in most cases the sale would fall through. It was clear that she didn't understand half the words, and that the reading level was way beyond her. Equally in demand and equally nonexistent were easy-to-read practical cookbooks. Both adults and girls as young as twelve were desperate for such a book. In my school volunteer work I had often encountered sixth-graders who were buying for and cooking for younger siblings with no idea of what to buy or of how to cook. I persuaded an experienced volunteer and excellent cook to write a book on a third-to-fourth-grade reading level which was not only a cookbook but also a buying and nutrition guide. We have yet to find a publisher, since the market is largely limited to poor people.

A market is there for low-reading-level books of all kinds, especially how-to books, since the urge for self-improvement is very great. In addition, there is a demand for popular books such as what we called "movie books," Ian Fleming, and especially movie books that have to do with black people, such as "To Sir with Love" and "In the Heat of the Night." This would be equally true with the other ethnic groups if, for example, there were movies about Puerto Ricans, Haitians, Cubans, etc. There is also a strong demand among adults and older adolescents for books on black history and biography.

As our clientele grew satisfyingly through the spring of 1968, we faced again the problem that we would need additional staff in the summer months ahead. Actually, we were short-staffed all year round for two reasons. First, our one small staff fulfilled *all* library functions—book selection, book ordering and processing, creation of publicity, distribution of publicity, recordkeeping, housekeeping, correspondence, and actual operation of the bookmobile. In a standard library situation, many of these functions are performed centrally, leaving the branch or bookmobile free to concentrate on operations. Second, while the educational level of the staff was an asset in relating to our public, it was a liability in the length of time it took to accomplish any clerical work and in the struggle for accuracy and completeness in recordkeeping.

We could let the clerical work slide or be sloppy, but in summer we had to have help with crowd control and publicity. Also, I was anxious to institute a story-telling program, and that too would require additional staff.

We had noticed the preceding summer that several students of junior-high age had spontaneously leaped aboard

Buttercup and helped out when they saw the need and the crowds were great. They had been able and enthusiastic assistants and had attracted others of their age to us.

With this memory in mind, I outlined a project called grandly "The Future Librarians of America." I would recruit (through the libraries) junior-high students from five junior high schools in our area who would help us as volunteers after school during the spring. The best of these we would hire to work for us part-time during the summer months. Using the geographical layout of our schedule, I picked a Monday school, Tuesday school, etc., so that my volunteers need help only one afternoon each week and need walk only a block or two from school to meet us.

I asked the Chase bank for $3,000 to fund the project, and they very generously backed me up.

I then talked to the librarians with varying success—two thought the children wouldn't consider volunteering, although they might be interested in a pay job in the summer; two thought the project was excellent but didn't seem to know their students very well, partly because they didn't live in the area and partly because both schools were having acute problems of their own. The fifth librarian lived in the area, knew her children well, and was enthusiastic. Her pupils became 80 percent of the Future Librarians. The remaining 20 percent we picked up from among our clientele. So the spring experience which I had hoped would be a training ground and winnowing ground was only semisuccessful.

Summer was another story. Our ten Future Librarians—five boys and five girls—were so enthusiastic that they proved a catalyst to the staff and the community. Despite the fact that they were often pelted with pebbles from rooftop children, set upon by neighborhood toughs, and forced by some inconsiderate summer-school teachers to deal with disruptive children whom the teachers preferred to ignore, they voluntarily came to Buttercup on their days off to help out wherever needed, much to the surprise and delight of the staff, since they had been hired to work for twenty hours a week only. The Spanish-speaking youngsters were especially helpful in telling stories in Spanish and in interpreting our services to those parents who were shy and hesitant. All the youngsters enjoyed making posters and other material for publicity, and some were very creative in decorating Buttercup. Their biggest thrill came on payday, when everyone at once rode in Buttercup to the Bedford branch of Chase to cash their checks. Three of them opened savings accounts, and all set aside money for school clothes.

The Future Librarians learned to perform all the tasks there were in connection with the project—processing, making out library cards, issuing and receiving books and pictures, and preparing and placing publicity material. However, their most exciting job was storytelling. We would send them out in groups of two in a two-block radius from our stop. Wherever there was a group of children, they would offer to tell a story and would then offer to bring the children back to Buttercup so they could borrow the book from which the story came. It usually wound up by their returning like the Pied Piper with a trail of children behind them, but not always.

It is interesting to realize that many library systems feel it is necessary for a person to have a college education to be a storyteller. These children, fourteen and fifteen, came from the neighborhood and attended the local schools. All were from minority groups, and most were from severely deprived homes, often with no father in the household. About half were quite far behind educationally. Yet all turned in a good responsible job, all proved to be good storytellers, and all were quick and inventive and imaginative. All gained clerical skills (as one boy put it, "Learning to file in strict alphabetical order will help me for the rest of my life"), and the requirement that all should be prepared to recommend books to Buttercup's patrons really got them reading and discussing books. All of them improved their reading as a result. It was fun, too, to hear how correct they were on the subject of reading for little kids, as they put it, and to hear their ideas on how kids should be brought up. All in all, they were a great help and inspiration and a joy to have around.

Much can be learned from the success of Buttercup. The story of that success must be traced to Mrs. Palmer's ride on the Swan Island ferry. As she compared the Swan Islander's enthusiasm to her memory of New York schoolchildren, she saw a need that had to be satisfied. The children of New York, too, needed the advantages of a bookmobile. The children of Swan Island "were part of the community." As Buttercup grew, it became a part of the community of Bedford-Stuyvesant and Bushwick.

It is unlikely that a call from a friend with $30,000 to spend will ever be received by many people. But this does not mean that the money cannot be raised. Mrs. Palmer's willingness to pursue a goal shows the second step in Buttercup's success. She tried to get the community to see the need and to stimulate a community effort toward a solution. The Public Library, the Board of Education, the director and trustees of the Public Library, the Hertz Company, and friends and acquaintances were contacted and the need explained. When the initial funding was secured and a board of trustees with adequate "political" power was selected, Buttercup could begin to operate.

Pools of volunteer talent and willingness can be found everywhere: among high-school and college-age students, young and older parents, and the retired.

An unheralded phase of student activism can be seen in student tutorial programs. Few colleges and universities are without offices and coordinators who mobilize undergrads and graduate students in an effort to learn, to communicate, and to do something relevant.

Some teacher-training programs use tutoring as a small part of the students' involvement with children and books. Tutorial programs can bring together the college students and children in a variety of instructional settings—in the home, at their school, on the university campus, in the park, or wherever it is appropriate.

Perhaps the chief value for the tutor is his opportunity to become sensitive to the needs of the learner. It may be his first opportunity to see and experience the difference between telling and teaching. Reality can be contrasted with theory. The child who learns slowly, the undernourished child, a concept too abstract for a ten-year-old—these problems are found and must be solved.

It is estimated that some 2,300 colleges and universities are represented in volunteer tutorial programs. College credit is often granted for this work. Departments of sociology, psychology, community services, public affairs, urban field service, medicine, education, and regional studies programs offer credit for tutorial work that ranges from one credit hour to thirteen hours each quarter.

A few selected examples of the programs which offer tutorial and volunteer assistance follow.

STUDENT CONCERN

Student Concern is a Florida-wide program of college and high-school student volunteers. Projects include 800 tutors in a city-wide program at Tampa (the Intensive Tutorial), with similar projects in Gainesville (Project Samson) and in Miami; a Big Brother program in Jacksonville; and summer day camps that provide recreational outlets for more than 400 youngsters near the University of Florida.

The Student Concern program has a Tallahassee-based administrative and coordinating staff and is supported by the state. The staff consists of a state coordinator and three assistant coordinators: (1) administrative affairs (fiscal); (2) state supportive services (liaison with state and other agencies, publicity, training materials, workshops, etc.); (3) local programs and development (direct contact and coordination with local coordinators and project directors). There are five regional developers. Their responsibilities include providing resource materials to organizations and campuses that wish to initiate programs and maintaining communication with established programs.

Many student government associations have set up clearinghouses for information and placement of students in these programs. In other cases, service and social fraternities, sororities, and clubs coordinate student manpower.

City fathers, county commissioners, leaders in state government, and university, junior-college, and high-school faculties and administrators not only support these students but also share their ideas and resources with them.

The activities of the Florida students vary from campus to campus. Many students are involved in tutoring. Tutoring can be described as a one-to-one, or one-to-small-group situation which presents an opportunity to make greater gains in learning a given subject matter, experience personal interaction, and provide for flexibility in teaching goals and teaching methods.

ARIZONA—TEMPE (COLLEGE TUTORIAL)

Dr. Nicholas Silvaroli and Dr. Marjorie Mertens of Arizona State University coordinate a program which brings elementary-school children to the university reading clinic for tutorial assistance.

Through agreement with the Phoenix School District

Board, ninety youngsters from the inner city are bussed each semester to ASU at least twice weekly for a minimum of two hours of tutoring on a one-to-one basis.

The tutors are upper-division ASU students in a College of Education class and some graduate students, many working on their doctorates.

The Reading Clinic includes fifteen individual instruction rooms equipped with one-way mirror glass and a speaker. The rooms are on both sides of a long narrow corridor, allowing both pupil and tutor to be under the watchful eye of faculty members and supervisors, without distracting from the tutoring. An ASU student with a problem presses a button to turn on a light in the corridor to let a supervisor know assistance is requested.

This program enables the tutor to receive expert help and guidance in working with children who may have some complicated reading problems. The child, of course, has the benefit of feeling that he is receiving special help when he works in a room with the facilities and materials available to a reading clinic on a college campus.

STOREFRONT STUDY

What would happen if you and your neighbors opened a reading-study center in a poverty neighborhood? Would the young children of the neighborhood come voluntarily to study and learn to read? That kind of center with volunteer help is cropping up in cities all over the country. Some of them are sponsored by churches or by the Urban League, but many get their impetus and support from a small group of individuals. Lenore Guttmacher wrote about the East Harlem Neighborhood Study Club and described it this way: *

* "Oasis on 100th Street," by Lenore G. Guttmacher, *The Wellesley* alumnae magazine, Vol. 54, No. 4.

This is an area known as "The Block," sometimes called the worst block in New York, a part of El Barrio. To me, it is a good block. I have worked here for over six years, as a volunteer, and from where I sit at my job, it is a good community. Perhaps I see only the best of it, the best people, young and old, all ages from the children to the parents and the grandparents.

True, The Neighborhood Study Club has iron bars securing its large plate-glass windows to protect its vulnerable exposure to the street corner on Second Avenue and on 100th Street. But what streetfront places don't? Inside it is cozy and bright, teeming with people and pleasant activity, children anywhere from six to sixteen or more. The walls are gay with maps and posters and pictures, many drawn by the students to celebrate special events or holidays.

The Study Club has never been vandalized, rocks have never been thrown at the windows, nor have there been any robberies, not even "incidents." The children and the neighborhood, both, have always treated it with respect. To them it is something of value because they have chosen it, themselves. The children come voluntarily to the Study Club. Nobody makes them, neither schoolteachers, nor parents nor Study Club personnel. There is a "belongingness" about it to everyone involved. Even Mr. Panteleros, the hot dog vendor at the street corner, is very much a part of the scene.

The atmosphere inside the Club is relaxed and friendly. Good discipline is maintained, as a rule, for the very reason that this kind of study club after school is entirely voluntary. The children come after school only because they want to, and they know the place is open to them until seven-thirty at night.

The whole thing began with the simple idea that schoolchildren living in crowded quarters, with little privacy or quiet in which to study, could use an after-school study club. Not a new idea except for this neighborhood, perhaps, where there was seldom anybody around who could help with homework.

And so, with a generous amount of money supplied through small foundations, an empty corner store was rented. Several teachers were engaged, a young community-liaison woman was employed, and the East Harlem Neighborhood Study Club was in business, nonprofit. Gradually, volunteer workers appeared, among them, myself.

I have seen the Study Club change and grow as I have seen the community change and grow. Everyone working here is particularly dedicated, dedicated in their attitude and, therefore, in their successful one-to-one relationship with the children. Now the Study Club is almost entirely community-oriented. Its director is the young woman originally engaged as its community-liaison worker, its tutors are local students, and its one "professional," a teacher, is the staff "resource" core. The Club's success with the children, always working with them on an individual basis, seems greater than ever.

One of our tutors is a young man I shall call Miguel. Bright and attractive, he is working his way through CCNY on his small salary at the Study Club. He excels at reading help with his young pupils because, while he takes no nonsense from them, he has a special kind of patience with them. He demands and holds their attention, and often when the hard work is over they flock around him like a mod Pied Piper, listening to the stories he tells, the jokes, whatever he has to say.

Another tutor, very much younger than Miguel, first came to the Club for after-school help. Withdrawn and so shy that he could scarcely speak loud enough to be heard in his reading lessons, Lorenzo was considered unteachable at school. Lenny, as he is now called, confessed to his non-English-speaking problem at the Study Club, learned quickly under the personal attention he got there, and blossomed miraculously in the easy, noncompetitive environment. Anxious to share his helpful experiences here, he has become one of our most dependable young tutors.

Other young people, some of them volunteers, proved to be extremely adept in tutorial capacities. Boys and girls tend to respond to their peers particularly well in this after-school study-club setting, I have observed.

After the first several years, we outgrew the one room and were able to rent the empty store next door to us. We converted its large open space into a special reading room so the youngsters could spill over into the second, quieter, room for their reading help. The Club was crowded, fifty or sixty children a day, sometimes noisy and always spirited.

Today is one of those days, the rooms bursting with earnest young spirits. When I finish with Celestina, Juanita comes over to me. "Can I read with you now, teacher, so I can go home to the baby for Mama? I've done my homework already and she's gotta go out."

Eddie comes next, but I hand him over to Bob, whom I know he prefers, and with whom he is making good progress. Bob has just come to the Study Club, after four years in Vietnam. He is a neighborhood hero, lives down the street, and the boys compete to work with him, as if some of his silent manliness might brush off on them. So, I take Alicia.

Reading is a struggle for her, but she is ambitious

and striving for a career, either to be "a secretary or a nurse or a beautician." She has scarcely missed a day at the Club, including the long hot summer mornings when we are open during July and August.

What makes the big difference in reading help here, compared to large schoolroom classes, is the individual attention each child receives. There is an added plus to this in that we all respond to that personal quality in a one-to-one relationship, the teacher as well as the pupil. Both of us learn.

Many children can advance two years in reading within a four-month period. Some make truly dramatic successes once the reading hurdle has been cleared, just as in any school, anywhere. Some, of course, make no progress at all, as can happen to certain children in any school anywhere.

The East Harlem Neighborhood Study Club will continue, I hope, growing, sending out new shoots, nourishing the present ones. The days are much too short. When I leave the Study Club I walk the few blocks to my home lost in thought. What makes our Study Club tick? What turns it on? In this area, an area like "The Block"? I think it is because it is such a positive force in such a negative environment. It is a glow in the dark.

In St. Louis, Missouri, a VISTA worker arranged with the public library to meet with young children to focus on black history and draw the children to books through that topic. He designed an eight-week summer program for Afro-American elementary-school children. The children met with group leaders in a branch of the St. Louis Public Library to hear about and discuss black history and culture.

Reading skills as such were not taught, but it was hoped that reading interests would be stimulated. Believing that children often read poorly because they aren't motivated by what they are given to read, the VISTA worker built a sense of identity in the children through books, films, and recordings by and about blacks. The group leaders hoped to stimulate the children to go from the discussion groups to the library shelves, with the help of a reading list prepared by the librarian.

In Montclair, New Jersey, Mrs. Genevieve Collins took a personal interest in the progress of her first-graders. She became concerned that her pupils weren't getting the best start in reading and decided to do something about it. "I saw that the school year wasn't enough to get the black children in my class started in reading," she explained, "so I went to the principal and asked him to keep my room open for six weeks in the summer. That was in 1966, and he agreed."

Mrs. Collins mailed a letter to the parents of all twenty-five children in her class. It was an invitation to send the youngsters back to school three mornings a week during half of the summer vacation. No pressure was applied and sixteen of the twenty-five pupils came and stayed for the full six weeks. Two high-school girls served as aides that first summer.

The results of this initial effort were so successful that an expanded program was held the next summer. This time, pupils in all three first grades were welcomed, and a corps of unpaid helpers was recruited. Twenty-eight children attended, and a matching number of volunteers responded. The one-to-one tutoring moved ahead rapidly. During the regular school year, teachers requested help for their pupils, and available volunteers soon numbered 128.

When each child reports to his tutor, he brings materials and a notebook from class. The notebook is the communicator in which the teacher suggests what she wants the volunteer to cover. At the end of the session, the volunteer enters comments on the pupil's progress that day.

Although teachers and tutors don't have frequent face-to-face contact, the volunteers do not function in a vacuum.

There are training sessions and conferences arranged by the coordinator in addition to the notebook communications. The program continued to grow and has since spread to other local schools.

PARENTS AND THE RETIRED

Some potential tutors are often overlooked. Parents are not usually asked to assist their own children as tutors in school. Retired persons are others who may not frequently come to mind as helpers. Both represent large groups of people that some projects are trying to involve.

A project in Orem, Utah, developed a parent-aide program. Despite the risk of having parents press their children too much in trying to teach them, the junior-high-school staff felt the program had potential. In parent orientation sessions they emphasized the need to let students read for practice and pleasure and suggested that this might improve parent-child relationships.

Students who were assigned to work with their own parents or a parent substitute alternated reading and physical education. Every other day they worked on reading.

Vocabulary development, word-attack skills, and comprehension were emphasized. A home reading program was set up. Parents kept a record of recreational reading and returned it to the school at the end of each term. All reading was on a level at which the student could read without adult assistance. Students were allowed to take small 35-mm projectors and reading films home. The films contained texts on a wide range of reading levels. This idea worked exceptionally well.

Junior-high students were recommended for parent-aide assistance if they scored below a certain level on a standard test. Parents of these students were contacted, and if one of them could not come to school to help, a substitute volunteer was assigned. The PTA and various service clubs supplied more than fifty volunteer mothers. Testing at the end of the year indicated students achieved an average of one and a half years' growth in reading; some made more than three years' progress. Evaluation of the program indicates that family relations also improved.

Experience and time are valuable commodities in education that often can be provided by retired persons. TEAM, Inc., a volunteer tutoring program sponsored by the Louisville, Kentucky, National Council of Jewish Women, the Volunteers Bureau, and the Kentucky Commission on Aging stands for *t*alent, *e*xperience, *a*bility, and *m*aturity. TEAM has involved retired and semiretired men and women in working with children in a school setting.

In the summer of 1965 the Louisville Board of Education accepted the TEAM plan and selected a city junior high school as a pilot project. The administration and most of the faculty were more than willing to try the program. It has since expanded gradually to additional junior high schools.

Participants range in age from mid-forties to late seventies. Stringent requirements have been established for TEAM members. Volunteers must understand that continuity is very important and be willing to work with children on a regular basis. They must understand that they are not replacing teachers, but are serving in a tutorial capacity only. On their part, the schools have been asked not to send children who are disciplinary problems. The volunteers are not equipped to act as disciplinarians, nor are they in the schools to act as baby-sitters for disruptive children.

TEAM volunteers work on a one-to-one, one-to-two, or small-group basis. Some work in the classrooms with the teacher. Others use any available place—the library, the lunchroom, the auditorium, the mimeographing room, or even a large closet.

TEAM volunteers have assisted in English, grammar, read-

ing, social studies, spelling, penmanship, home economics, con-
versational German and French, art, and wood- and metalwork.
No volunteer worked less than two hours a week. Many worked
a full day, some two or three days a week, and a few every day.

TEAM fills a dual purpose. The volunteers know they are
doing an important job, and the children gain from association
with the volunteers. Attitude change is considered as important
as grade change in this project. Many of the students have
shown a marked change in their attitude toward the future and
toward schooling because of the interest of TEAM volunteers.

Students have expressed gratitude for the extra help and
attention they have received. Once convinced that the volunteer was there because of love and not pay, they looked forward to their sessions. They have exchanged notes at Christmas
and at the end of the school year. For many, relationships are
formed which last long after they have left junior high.

Special workshops and orientation sessions were given to
volunteers, and periodic volunteer-faculty meetings were held
in all the schools. These gave the teachers and volunteers the
opportunity to meet, to discuss the children and their needs,
and to work out future assignments. One school formed its own
motor pool. Mothers in the PTA, eager to be involved in
TEAM, picked up nondriving volunteers, brought them to
school, and drove them home.

The success of the program is measured in many ways.
The newspapers, for example, saw merit in it and gave generous space to TEAM. The *National Aging* magazine did a picture story on TEAM volunteers. As a result, TEAM leaders
have corresponded with people in many cities about initiating
TEAM programs in their schools. Most volunteers who started
with TEAM in 1965 are still active. Student failures have been
reduced. Many children who were discouraged and disheart-
ened because they thought no one cared have learned there are
people who do care and who give of themselves. Older people

who thought that their useful days were over have learned that they are needed and have helped some children feel needed, too. These are all indications of success that should be counted.

To schedule volunteers, a library-card jacket—one for each volunteer—was tacked on a large bulletin board in each school under the day (or days) the volunteer was to be there. The volunteer's name, address, telephone number, subject to be tutored, time at school, and room or area where he was to be working were printed on the front of each jacket. A three-by-five white card held the specific information needed such as: names of pupils to see the volunteer, what time they were to come, name of the teacher, or sessions volunteer would miss because of illness, etc. Some cards had to be changed each week because of schedule changes involving individual pupils, but others did not have to be changed often, especially where the volunteer was going into the room to work directly under the teacher. From an administrative point of view, having the volunteers assigned to a teacher made the job much easier. The teacher then directed all specific activities.

A special pass was given to pupils who were to meet with volunteers each day. This seemed to be the most reliable way to make sure the pupils were on time for the tutoring session. Teachers working directly with tutors also received a reminder.

The TEAM experience has shown that a school system with a lay advisory board or a group of citizens interested in organizing retired people could administer a similar program.

MASS MOBILIZATION
FOR LOW-INCOME STUDENTS

Because low-income areas have a large proportion of poor readers, it seems clear that significant additional help is needed.

A PACE group (Planned Action for Community Education) in Wichita, Kansas, decided that one volunteer per student was needed. There were 4,880 students in the target area chosen, and PACE went after 4,875 volunteers. Not every student needs a tutor, but he has access to one or more if he wants assistance in several areas. PACE's main effort to achieve better education for low-income children is through this mobilization, training, and direction of volunteers.

Volunteers try to see that a child succeeds at a reading task several times a week and that school work is interesting and connected to a child's experience. They use creative techniques to help children learn, provide new experiences for children, and serve as a link between teacher, child, and family.

PACE secured the assistance of teachers and professors in referring pupils, in working with tutors, and in training and evaluation. Others assisted the PACE recruitment offices, giving speeches, etc. Study centers were often supervised by volunteers. Volunteers came from junior high schools, high schools, colleges, Family Consultation Office, Mental Health Office, Wichita Guidance Center, Extension Services, Bell Telephone, McConnell Air Force Base, churches, and the business community.

Learning to read, to add and subtract, or to do any of the school activities is not pleasurable to many children. It is next to impossible for children deprived of food, housing, and a vision of the future. Thus, while the PACE program is designed to aid children in school, the emphasis is on the development of the child's self-image.

PACE recognized the lack of professional preparation in their volunteers, but insisted that it takes no training to recognize the dignity of all human beings.

The growing pains of a program with limited resources taught the PACE staff some lessons. Staff involvement in a summer program and other activities unrelated to the tutoring program was a handicap. In some cases VISTA volunteers were used as supervisors, and this weakened administrative control in the neighborhoods. School tutoring suffered from insufficient tutor-teacher contact and exchange, and at-home tutoring from a lack of communication between supervisors and staff. A lack of continuing training of volunteers in specific skills and inadequate follow-up on problems and success led to irregular attendance of tutors and loss of volunteers. There were also insufficient materials and equipment to assist and train tutors in dealing with the problems of the poor.

Identification of these weaknesses enabled the PACE staff to improve. The number of tutors was reduced to six hundred, and a pool of tutors is controlled as selective recruitment and appropriate training absorb them.

The PACE staff is now service-oriented rather than product-oriented. The staff serves in a resource and advisory capacity rather than as active organizers. Organizers are recruited for specific jobs so that tutors can be trained in specific reading skills.

An evaluation effort was developed so that program results could be assessed systematically and more effectively. Data related to school achievement, attitude, discipline, attendance, and extracurricular activities are collected.

The difficulties identified by the PACE staff, the decision to change in light of their findings, and the evaluation effort offer other volunteer programs potent ideas. Program improvement can occur rationally when information is gathered and the needs of the program are put into focus.

2 ❧ Preschool Programs

THE YEARS from one to six or seven are seen by most learning specialists as the most important. What happens to the child then shapes so much of the way he thinks and feels that it is crucial for us to give him our best attention.

During the preschool years a child develops a sense of who he is and how valuable he is. He begins to sense how he should react to the world around him. Can he afford to be open and exploring, or should he put out cautious feelers to avoid pain? He hears sounds and learns to imitate them. If he is encouraged to communicate, he wants to learn the sound system rapidly because he sees that it leads to pleasure and advantage. The more language he learns, the more he can command and control. On the other hand, if he hears little language and is not encouraged to communicate, he explores his world with sight and touch but does not practice with words.

Language and concept development are intimately related. Without language a child cannot easily communicate or learn whether his impressions are similar to others. Language demands great amounts of practice. Without practice, words and patterns come haltingly or not at all. As the child grows and plays with other children, he begins to form an impression of himself. He compares what he can do with what other children do, and his self-image and self-confidence take shape. Is he successful? Is he loved? Is he told that he is valuable? All of these impressions prepare him for activity in school and in life. More importantly, they begin to set him in the way he will respond and think.

The child's capacity for learning and change during the early years is great, and it is necessary to take full advantage of it. Learning need not be formal schooling, but the opportunities for learning language, concepts, self-impressions, and patterns of thinking should be positive and as open as circumstances will allow. That's where volunteers can help.

Nursery schools. There are, of course, established schools to aid and guide development of the preschool child. Some may be little more than baby-sitting centers, but there are many more that help the child develop the mental, social, and psychological capabilities that will aid him in school, especially in learning to read and communicate. (We don't want to give the impression that nothing else happens in nursery schools, but this discussion is aimed toward activities and programs that assist reading, and therefore we have chosen what fits the theme of this book.)

Because we are concerned with programs in which volunteers and aides help with reading, we will not describe in detail nationally known schools, such as Montessori, but rather will describe programs where the layman is likely to be involved, such as cooperative nursery schools and Head Start programs. Nationally franchised schools train their personnel, and local nursery schools and Head Start programs orient their lay help and provide a sense of direction. Volunteers need a few specific principles and activities that they learn to do well. For example, it would benefit nursery-school workers to know and apply some of the following:

1. Language should start with concrete experience wher-

ever possible. Don't describe a *cone;* hand a plastic, wooden, or paper cone to the child and let him handle it as part of teaching him the word, and its relation to sphere, cylinder, tube, and so on. What can you use it for? Where do you see cones? Can you draw one?

2. Social relationships are also best understood when seen in some concrete form. Visits to municipal stations is one way. Policemen, firemen, workers, mothers, fathers, children, and so on, can be put together in a toy city which the children play with. Or children can take roles that they already know, and act them out in creative dramatics, each child thus learning from others what different people do. (The adult is always available as a consultant and guide, of course.)

3. There is no clear-cut set of experiences and no divinely inspired sequence of activities a child must go through to learn to read. Children can explore many things, concepts, and relations in different sequences and still learn to speak fluently and read with comprehension. Thus, encouraging children to explore, to think aloud, and to ask questions are more ways the adult assists in growth.

4. Language develops best through use in interesting activities. While painting or coloring, the child learns about colors, sizes, shapes, designs, and distances. While building or playing games, he learns about numbers, number concepts, success and failure, winners, and those that come in second. The adult explains, provides, demonstrates, and shows how.

5. Thinking patterns can be prompted by questions the adult asks. If a child is retelling a story, the adult can stimulate his thinking by asking questions beginning with "how" and "why." How did you think he got to the moon? Why did he want to go there? How would you have ended the story? Why would you want to be Jack instead of the goose that laid the golden egg?

Especially for children from areas deprived of money or verbal stimulation, the early child centers, nursery schools, and

Head Start programs enable the child to use his early years to learn language, develop valuable concepts, build positive attitudes toward learning and society, and establish patterns of thinking and acting that will serve him throughout his life. That sounds like much more than reading, and it is, but reading is intimately linked with the language, concepts, attitudes, and thinking patterns that a child has as he approaches the printed page.

Nursery schools and related programs are places where the child should discover that learning can be fun. In a sense, he ought not to be conscious that he is going to school—in the traditional sense of schooling. At this age, learning should be an unpressured atmosphere of adventure, discovery, and sharing. Order is needed, of course, and it can arise from a sense of respect for others. A desirable learning atmosphere does not just happen. Both the professional and the lay staffs need concepts and attitudes to develop that kind of school. The professional staff should have the responsibility for planning and organizing the program. The lay staff, with training, can participate in activities that it has been prepared for. Together they can exercise creative talents for the benefit of the child.

Some early childhood programs have well-prepared material and equipment and follow patterns that work. Montessori schools, for example, encourage children to explore the world with their senses before they are expected to engage in more abstract tasks. Some programs move directly into the development of abstract functions, feeling that it is necessary to prepare the children for first grade. It seems important, therefore, for early-childhood workers to have a sense of direction; that is, know what goals they are trying to achieve and not merely work with children on a day-to-day basis. This sense of direction cannot happen with a "walk-on" staff. Each member of the staff needs orientation for the part he will have in the school.

An unprecedented number and variety of approaches to

the development of an atmosphere where reading flourishes are now being used for preschools, elementary and secondary age groups, and adults.

Many of them are described in this chapter. Some support what is being done in the regular school curriculum, some supplement the school program, and others parallel formal instruction in separate settings.

SAMPLE PRESCHOOL PROGRAMS

At this end of the spectrum we find some programs devoted directly to preparing children to enter a school reading situation and others more concerned with the long-term prevention of failure in reading and communication. Preparation and prevention: the distinction may not always be clear. Early preparation could be a means of preventing failure, but if the program works on specific skills and concepts to enable the child to step more easily into the school program, we shall categorize it as preparation. Many experimental nursery schools sponsored by public school systems fall into this category.

Sesame Street. Sesame Street uses television to prepare children to enter the world of books and school concepts. The letters of the alphabet, sound-symbol associations, numbers, vocabulary, and similar skills related to first-grade schooling are part of Sesame Street. It is dressed in a nonschool format with clowns and flashing words, but it has obvious links to first-grade books. In many communities, like Mansfield, Ohio, for example, Sesame Street Centers have been formed and meet in churches, activity centers, and libraries and encourage volunteers to use the guides published by Sesame Street as follow-ups.

Parent Involvement. There are programs, such as one in Skamania County, Washington, where volunteers go into homes to try to convince parents to read with their preschool children. It is an attempt by the school district to accomplish the following:

1. To aid the parents to recognize the physical, social, and mental development processes of preschool children.

2. To assist the parents in improving their children's vocabulary development, auditory and visual discrimination, eye-to-hand coordination, and spatial-relationship perceptions.

3. To help parents instruct their children by utilizing multimedia reading materials at home. These materials include filmstrips, tapes, educational games, and study prints provided by the project.

4. To increase parent involvement in the schooling of their children by classroom observation, attendance at extracurricular activities, and contacts with professional staff members.

Parents and children are organized into twenty-six neighborhood centers with four to six parents per center. Each center has a volunteer parent coordinator and an assigned adviser who is a teacher. A home-school parent aide visits the centers and parents to provide instruction in using the materials and to suggest methods for working with children. Parents have access to educational games and equipment. Toy laboratories have been established in each school to add to the student's experience and knowledge about many things.

The program's value is in creating parent awareness of a readiness for reading and in enabling the teacher and parent to cooperate for the child's benefit. It has significant possibilities for getting home and school together, especially in poverty neighborhoods where parents and teachers are often at odds. The neighborhood centers bring people together in more comfortable circumstances and relieve the anxiety many poverty parents have about going to school. This program has possibilities for upgrading the entire family by getting the parent to focus on the child's learning. More than one has improved his own reading through exercises he practices with his children.

One of the drawbacks is that volunteers and parents may be expected to understand some concepts that require more time and background than they have. It is a risk, but not one that should discourage a school from trying it, or volunteers from participating.

REACH THE FAMILY

Libraries also are trying to reach the entire family through programs for children. Almost every family is interested in helping youngsters learn what they need for success in school. The St. Paul, Minnesota, Public Library, for example, believes family encouragement forms an integral part of the picture of the young reader. Staff members who participate in the library's community programs must be impressed personally with the pleasures and importance of reading and be interested in passing on their enthusiasm to the families they serve. Their theme is: "Interest and enthusiasm are contagious."

The library wants adults (and children, too) to believe the library can meet their needs, and that it really wants to. Developing the attitude of the staff, therefore, plays a key role in the success of its programs. Samples of efforts to involve the entire family include the following:

Mothers' Morning Out. This is a program designed to reach housewives. The women may bring preschool children for a story hour. One staff person talks to the mothers about books and library services while one or two others work with children telling them stories and using books and demonstrations. Books are available for the women and children to take out. This program is taken into neighborhoods, community centers, and churches. It is advertised through local agencies by newsletters and fliers. It continues on a once-a-week basis for five to eight weeks.

Work with Volunteers. Traveling workshops in puppetry reach scouts, teens, and school volunteers who are shown how to make puppets for use with their pupils. The workshops include ideas on various kinds of playlets and storytelling.

Sidewalk Service (Summer Program). A Ford van is used to carry paperback books into neighborhoods. The most successful approach has been to work through a definite contact, such as a woman who has taken part in one of the library programs. She invites women from the neighborhood to her house. They are encouraged to bring their young children. A library staff member talks about the library and books. A story hour is held for the children, and books are available to check out. The van is used for *promotion* only, so no regular stops are made. It is part of the library's effort to get the entire family, and especially young children, to see books and reading as an important and happy part of their lives.

Fire-Station Stops. An effort to reach fathers comes through stops at city fire stations to tell about the library and to have firemen get cards and take books from the van. The van carries the usual paperback collection as well as additional books considered of special interest to men. Unless the men are called, they are a captive audience. Many men feel they are too busy to read, so the staff stresses that books can be of practical value, even time-savers, in doing a project around the house or in a hobby.

A similar emphasis can be seen in the New York City area. The Queens Borough Public Library has developed a picture-book program for three-to-five-year-olds that involves their parents. The philosophy of this program is embodied in the slogan: "While their children are getting a Head Start to Reading . . . PARENTS have a chance to add to their own store of knowledge." Children are included in readiness-to-read activities while parents view films, engage in discussions, read, and learn how to participate in the education of their children.

These programs correctly emphasize making parents aware of the language development and the attitude toward books their children need to assist them in learning to read.

Many libraries are now conducting preschool programs outside their walls. The Free Library of Philadelphia, for example, uses storytelling to motivate children to books and reading. Storytelling at schools, settlement houses, parks, playgrounds, hospitals, churches, camps, street corners, etc., for preschool to eighth grade is used throughout the city by the children's libraries. The library extends its influence by training teachers, teacher aides, parents, and students in the art of storytelling and reading aloud.

FORMAL SCHOOLING FOR
THE PRESCHOOLER

More and more private and public schools have formal programs for preparing young children for reading and related skills and attitudes. Volunteers can find work in these schools as well as the more informal approaches to preparation. It should be noted, however, that the formal schools are usually operated by specially trained personnel, and they may demand more training time for volunteers than other programs, including those in established or "alternate" schools.

Ben Mott School. In Chattanooga, an independent grocer, Ben Mott, and a group of churches and neighbors joined in establishing a preschool for children who live in the area near Mr. Mott's store. They organized a program for children two to five years old. In addition to the conventional preschool activities such as storytelling, painting, music, creative handwork, games, free play, and field trips, the program stresses two or three short study periods per day for instruction in language, numbers, and reading.

Most of the children are disadvantaged blacks who pay no tuition. There are a few disadvantaged white children from adjoining neighborhoods who pay no tuition, and a few children whose parents want them to have the experience and who pay tuition.

The school is staffed by a paid director and five part-time teachers, all of whom are college graduates with experience in early-childhood education. In addition, there are approximately twenty-five volunteers, each working one morning a week. Finances are obtained from churches, individuals, and the Community Action Program.

The director who was hired had worked with two professors at the University of Illinois, Carl Bereiter and Siegfried Englemann, who were developing a program for teaching disadvantaged children. They found that these children become isolated because of severe limitations in language usage and that although they master language adequate for maintaining social relationships and for meeting their material needs, they do not learn to use language for obtaining and transmitting information, for monitoring their own behavior, and for carrying on verbal reasoning. In short, they fail to master the uses of language which are of primary importance in school. These uses include the ability to describe, to inquire, to explain, to compare, to analyze, to deduce, and to test. These are qualities of language necessary for academic success. It has been demonstrated that a child who fails to master these uses has little chance to succeed in school.

By the age of three or four, children seriously behind in the development of aptitudes for success in school must catch up or they will enter school with handicaps that spell failure. If they are to catch up, they must progress faster than normal. A preschool program that provides the usual opportunities for learning cannot be expected to produce learning at above normal rates. Some selectivity is necessary. For Bereiter and Englemann this selectivity involved discovering particular language problems and concentrating on overcoming them. They put their selective activities in a set of materials that follows a programmed learning approach. The Mott School, using this system, zeros in on concepts believed necessary for first-grade achievement and helps the disadvantaged catch up.

HEAD START

Head Start programs encompass all kinds of educational programs. From one city to another one can find those that seem to be following a philosophy similar to Montessori and those that lean toward that of Bereiter-Englemann, and those that are varying shades between. Local direction is one of the strong features of Head Start programs, and they offer lay people plenty of opportunity for participating in preschool education.

Most Head Start programs strive to serve children through the talents of neighborhood people, especially those who have some special training. Country dwellers as well as city dwellers have Head Start programs. The programs are intended for poverty-afflicted children, and city children have no corner on that. Invariably, too, Head Start programs hire aides from the neighborhoods where the program is. They are trained, as are volunteers, to carry on those tasks that fit into the framework of the program. In Columbus, Indiana, for example, aides serve in rural communities and teach children games, cooking, art, and music and take them on field trips: all combine to instill a desire for learning and to create the attitude that school is a "fun" place.

In Florida there is a statewide Head Start program for the children of migrants. Aides and volunteers use films called "Let's Learn Language" to acquaint the children with standard phrases and sentences used in the primary grades. The films feature puppets who talk to the children and encourage them to respond. These materials are used in the Ben Mott School and are arranged so the child masters the skills he needs before he is required to use them. The language, reading, and arithmetic programs (arithmetic is also taught as a language) are designed to support, enrich, and enhance each other so that each child's progress is at the fastest possible rate.

After the films, volunteers and aides use puppets and pictures to get the children to practice the phrases that were introduced. Some of the practice is done in groups, and some on a one-to-one basis. The volunteer plays a key role by giving each individual sufficient practice to make the language pattern part of what the child can say without thinking. The opportunity to respond regularly to an adult also removes any fear the poverty child may have in speaking to an adult—especially one who may seem to live a quite different life from his.

PUBLIC SCHOOL PRESCHOOLS

Public school kindergartens are fixtures of many public school systems, but few communities have public school nursery schools yet. Where they exist or are being tested, volunteer and teacher-aide assistance is being sought to establish a favorable adult-child ratio and to give young children many opportunities to hear and use language, and to hear and use concepts or abstractions that will serve them in school, especially in learning to read.

Fresno, California. Public schools are trying to prepare Spanish-speaking children for first-grade reading through a special preschool program. There are not more than fifteen children per class, with one teacher, one teacher aide, and at least one volunteer. They help the children develop language and concepts for first grade through activities which include experiences in language (finger plays, telephone); music (singing, rhythmic and interpretive physical reactions such as marching, being bears, being trees in the wind); arts and crafts (finger painting, clay); science (living things, magnets); health and safety (rest, nutrition, cleanliness); and games and educational toys (puzzles, Tinker Toys). The California climate also permits major emphasis on the outdoors as a classroom, and the curriculum includes walks and bus trips. These activities are designed: (1) to develop a functional English vocabulary by presenting new words in the context of the student's activities; (2) to encourage the child to speak freely in English; (3) to introduce the child to standard sentence structure through example; (4) to stress listening and speaking skills; and (5) to emphasize articulation by example rather than correction.

Teachers use a list of "English Sounds for Which There Is No Equivalent in Spanish," along with a list of 58 finger plays appropriate for each sound. For example:

i   him, this, his.
        This sound has *no* equivalent in Spanish. There will
        be a tendency to pronounce these words as *heem,
        thees, hees.*

j   jump, judge.
        This sound has no counterpart in Spanish and must
        be taught. *J* is sometimes substituted for *y* in such
        words as *yes, yellow.*

Oakland, California, used similar activities for disadvantaged English-speaking children. They paid special attention to improvement of language skills and stimulation of interest and curiosity.

Improvement of the language skills of the Oakland children was undertaken in several ways. The "Housekeeping Corner" was used for telephone conversations and other forms of dramatic play. Children were encouraged to name and talk about the foods provided for them at "Snack Time." "Listening Center" activities included hearing tapes and records of music and stories. Language Master materials were used to teach the children to recognize their names and to develop a basic vocabulary, while the daily language period reinforced language skills through such activities as retelling stories and playing games which emphasized distinguishing sounds of words. Finally, daily opportunities for children to talk with preschool staff personnel and parent volunteers expanded and reinforced their language skills.

Excursions to local places of interest, music and rhythm activities, science experiments with magnets and floating objects, classroom experience with animals, and the opportunity to plant seeds and watch flowers and vegetables grow are a few of the many program activities designed to stimulate the interest and curiosity of the children.

Oakland found that by preparing specific lesson plans, such as the following, lay aides could be used to give many children a chance to listen and express their own story endings.

Literature Lesson
Purpose: To let children become familiar with the
    Mother Goose nursery rhymes.
Material: *Flannel Story—Little Miss Muffet*
Instruction: Tell the rhyme using the flannel characters.
    Retell and let the children help finish parts, e.g.,
    "and down came a _____."
Variation 1—Let a child put the appropriate pieces on
    a flannel board as the story is told.

Variation 2—Let a child tell the rhyme as the teacher or
    another child puts on the pieces.

Variation 3—Talk about the rhymes and help children
    think about how many things happened in the story.
    1. Miss Muffet sat down.
    2. She ate.
    3. Spider came.
    4. Miss Muffet ran away.

This should clarify the story and the sequence.
To emphasize this, mix up the story and have the children tell you what is wrong, e.g., "The spider sat down
to eat, and Miss Muffet came and frightened him."

PREVENTION PROGRAM

As indicated earlier, there are child-education specialists who
feel that what happens during his early life, especially fifteen
months to three years, is critical to a child's language and concept development. Lack of language stimulation during that
time could leave a child at age five with a deficit he must work
mightily to overcome, if he can at all. For that reason, there
are many programs, of interest to volunteers, focusing on those
critical months and aimed at preventing language and reading-
related deficits.

To the untrained eye, the activities of these programs may
not look like reading, but the same could be said of many typical kindergarten programs. Needless to say, creating an attitude
favorable to learning and books, offering opportunities to expand experience and to discuss and to feel language and its
results contribute significantly to the child's later performance.

Operation Home Start. In Waterloo and Cedar Rapids,
Iowa, for example, there is an effort to acquaint parents with the

values of toys in the early years. Called Operation Home Start, the program lends toys and other materials designed to aid a child in developing skills in such things as motor coordination and color recognition. Trained volunteers visit the homes, taking toys and materials to show parents how they are useful. They also demonstrate how to encourage the child to explore and investigate.

Home Start is now an integral part of the public school system. However, it was conceived and initiated by the local chapter of the American Association of University Women (AAUW), which supplies many of the volunteers.

The Home Start project reminds us that playing is learning for the young child. Later, play may become a chance for relaxation. The very young child, however, learns constantly from interesting and sometimes challenging toys and playtime materials. A set of building blocks, for example, enables the child to learn to stack, create, build, and throw. Given a hint of what can be done with a toy, most children will explore endlessly and will ask questions and explain if the adult shows interest. Learning does not necessarily mean schooling, and parents or volunteers should not think of the early years as a time for schooling.

HIGH SCHOOL GIRLS VOLUNTEER

In Miami, Florida, the Edison-Little River Economic Opportunity Program works with children aged eighteen to thirty months.

Betty Lou Barbieri, area director of EOP, said, "I kept reading that one should work with babies, and one Harvard professor even wrote about prenatal education. We have a child-care center for two-and-a-half-year-olds to five-year-olds, but I wanted to start even younger, to give a 'head start' to very young children in the area in an attempt to increase their ability to learn and use language." She read a report from the Cornell Research Program in Early Childhood Education that "listening to stories may be more than a pleasure; it may be a very important key to a child's ability to learn to use language."

EOP decided to try a Visiting Reader Program, in which girls between the ages of fourteen and eighteen would go into the homes of very young children to read to them. Both the readers and the listeners came from low-income families in the area.

The girls were screened for reliability, desire to work with young children, maturity, and interest. Each was assigned to a child to read to for one hour, twice a week. For this work, they received a minimum hourly wage.

The children were selected by social-service assistants on the basis of recommendations from elementary schools. Brothers and sisters of Head Start and Child Opportunity Center children were given priority.

The readers were trained in a two-week period. The first few days were spent building the girls' self-confidence. A film about story reading helped them to understand their role. They made a list of things—beads, plastic toy animals, paper, hand puppets, ring stacks, etc.—that they could carry to draw the children's attention to books and conversation. Concrete objects are usually necessary to lead the young child to deal with the abstractions in story books. The more immature the child, the more it is necessary to start with concrete experience. The public library provided each storyteller unlimited borrowing privileges.

An evaluation of the project by a VISTA observer noted:

1. One or two girls had to be replaced when they couldn't cope with the responsibility, but most of them blossomed.

2. The girls have seen improvement. At first, the children were passive. Now they take an active part in the reading—repeating words and pointing to the pictures. If the word or

story is about a wagon, for example, the child will bring his own wagon into the room. The child also will imitate animal sounds from the pictures shown.

3. The children are grasping basic concepts. The girls have been using shape/color puzzles.

4. The children can count and distinguish various physical features such as eyes and ears, and are able to pick out one object from several.

5. The girls have found that if they come every other day the child responds better.

6. The girls have shown a marked increase in their understanding of children. They will leave if the child is cranky and crying, realizing that, as one of the girls said, "You can't teach a tired baby a thing; you can't even play with it." They never force the children, realizing the futility of such a move.

7. The increase in their self-confidence is amazing. They are willing to train a new group of storytellers, although when it was first mentioned, their hesitation was obvious. Now they're expounding their own view of training.

8. The parents have expressed praise for the program. They've spoken of the children's interest in having them read books left by the girls. The parents' approval is demonstrated when they try to keep older brothers and sisters quiet when the girls are working.

Informal though that evaluation is, it shows a concern to assess the behavior or attitude of primary participants, storyteller, infant, and parent, who said in effect: listening, language, and books are important.

ATTITUDE DEVELOPMENT

From its inception, the Perry Preschool in Ypsilanti, Michigan, was a school-organized, district-sponsored effort to effect positive change in the capability of culturally deprived children, hoping it would lead to academic success and social adjustment in the elementary grades. This program took place in a specially prepared facility that made it possible for many adults to work with the children, and it included a parent-education component.

Four preschool teachers operated a morning program divided into two instructional periods separated by a refreshment time. The early instruction period was for an hour in the largest of the school's three rooms. Each teacher was stationed in one of the four "area teaching" divisions of the classroom: arts and crafts, housekeeping, preacademic, and block activities. The children were free to select any of the four centers. A child could participate or observe as long as he liked and could move from one area to another. Each teacher's plans included activities which could be adapted to the individual children in her center. The activities were designed to emphasize the following: sensory perception, language development, memorization, and concept development.

The second period was more highly structured. The children were divided into two groups, approximately twelve students per group, based on learning ability. Two teachers worked with each group, making the pupil-teacher ratio 6:1. The groups met for about twenty minutes in two small separate classrooms adjacent to the larger room.

Lessons were designed to teach a particular skill or concept which was missing from the children's behavior in order to help build a foundation for future learning.

The afternoon program was home-based. Its purposes were to involve the mother in the education of her child, to demonstrate the process of teaching, and to tutor the child on a one-to-one basis. The home visits also offered an opportunity for the teacher to become more cognizant of the child's deficits, thereby enabling her to work more effectively in the classroom.

Some afternoons were used for field trips in which parents and volunteers participated. On other afternoons, skill development was stressed. For example: visual training (identifying objects, colors, forms, letters); fine-motor coordination necessary for writing (tracing dotted lines); auditory discrimination essential in learning to read (listening to records, responding to instructions, imitating and classifying sounds); premath training (counting silverware); and general science training (planting seeds, making Jell-O). The area of emphasis and the activities were varied to suit the individual child and home situation.

HOW LIBRARIES CAN HELP

The freedom and creativity displayed by libraries in this context are illustrated by the Fair Oaks Branch Library at Stockton, California. In 1965, the librarian, Mrs. Virginia Struhsaker, organized a Library Preschool Program under the sponsorship of OEO. The program focused on reading readiness and general school readiness for culturally deprived children from minority groups.

Four groups of twenty preschool children received five weeks' training in eleven 1½-hour class periods the first summer. The project with these eighty children was expanded with $9,000 in OEO funds for one year. The basic term was set at eleven weeks of two 1½-hour classes. Sixteen groups of twenty children each were trained during the full year. The program was re-funded for the following three years, also. Most of the budget went for personnel and basic materials. Three part-time library aides recruited in the neighborhood have been on the OEO staff to participate in the preschool training sessions.

The library's regular staff planned and directed the program and participated as needed. Many volunteers aided. In 1968, using accumulated experience and materials, the program further expanded by sending traveling story hours for pre-schoolers to neighborhood centers, migrant camps, and day-care centers in the area with as many as eight special programs per week.

When federal funds dried up, the city of Stockton granted additional personnel (one half-time library assistant and one part-time page) to continue the preschool library program. It was then feasible to conduct three sessions—fall/winter, spring, and summer—with three classes of twenty preschoolers each meeting twice weekly for eleven weeks. The preschoolers were about evenly divided among black, Mexican-American, and white, almost all being from families with low educational, economic, and opportunity outlook. Parents, brothers and sisters, and other relatives frequently were present at the lessons. Seventy percent of more than 1,300 preschoolers have graduated to receive their free book to start their home reading library.

The program included play with carefully chosen toys followed by stories, poetry, filmstrips, movies, puppet plays, and records. Games, finger plays, songs, counting, coloring, show-and-tell, and occasional crafts are interspersed.

Three half-time pages and assistants and many volunteers carried out the program.

The branch librarian plans and directs the program and participates to some degree, although most of the preparation, program time, and traveling story time is handled by the pre-school staff.

Volunteers have been used extensively and frequently—mostly drawn from preschool family and neighborhood people. They help set up the room for programs and straighten up afterward, prepare materials, help with games, occasionally prepare refreshments, and assist in advertising the program.

Major equipment purchased for the program includes a movie projector and screen; a filmstrip projector; a portable phonograph and records; a steel rack of cardboard boxes to hold puppets, toys, and other small objects; a filing case for flannelgraphs and filmstrips; a flannelgraph board; a considerable number of short black-and-white reels for children—many purchased at a close-out sale very cheaply; and a film rack for the reels.

Books, toys, and materials have been kept separately from the regular books to attract the children's attention. A wide variety of educational toys and play toys have been accumulated. Almost 900 books are included in this special collection. Toys, filmstrips, flannelgraphs, puzzles, and puppets have been extensively used in the program. Supplies are of the usual paper, crayons, felt markers, paper cups, tissues, yarn, etc.

Leaflets in English and Spanish were distributed throughout the neighborhood to advertise the programs. Announcements at PTA and other school meetings and at church meetings were made. Radio spot announcements have been used, too. But word-of-mouth advertising by preschool parents has helped about as much as anything.

The popularity of this program, the demand for admittance, the support of parents, the response of kindergarten teachers in nearby schools, and the attention of educational groups in the city and county and from far afield attest to the success of this program. The fact the city of Stockton renewed the program with funds in a year when it was not generally granting personnel requests showed local support. All who have participated agreed the program has a place in the educational work of the library in reaching out to help deprived areas.

3 ⚹ Elementary-School Programs

THERE ARE endless examples of how to help the elementary-school-age child. Some reflect the concern of dynamic individuals who practically run their own school, while others, run by agencies, carefully direct how volunteers act. All, however, are concerned about helping the child through the critical years. Some program ideas for agencies and individuals can be found in the descriptions that follow.

A school for failures. Have you ever wanted to start your own school? One way is to walk into a public housing development for blacks and announce you are going to start a free elementary school. You are especially interested in children who have not succeeded in regular school. Tell the kids playing in the courtyards; knock on doors and tell the parents; let the grocer know, and the man who runs the dime store. Be sure to tell them it doesn't matter what their religion is—even though the school will be in a recently closed parochial school building. And even though you are wearing a nun's habit, tell them all those things, because you are a nun in South Bend, Indiana, with a desire to help poor children, and you want to show that children from poverty neighborhoods can learn and will enjoy school if given help. And, by the way, do all this without substantial backing. Lease your school for $1,000 a year plus maintenance and utilities; beg your books and equipment from local merchants; and get some students from Notre Dame and other local colleges to act as volunteer tutors and fund raisers. Every afternoon after school, drive to local markets and ask for bread and ham salad and lettuce and milk or juice so your pupils can have a free snack and lunch on the next day.

Not many of us could manage all that, but that is exactly what Sister Marita did for slum children at South Bend. Between sixty and ninety children each year attended primary grades at her school instead of another school where they had not succeeded. The emphasis was on reading, because Sister Marita had strong feelings about reading being the key to success in the elementary school. She devised her own method and materials, and by playing phonics games and dictating their own stories to volunteers, the children got their first practice in reading.

One of the rooms in the school was turned into a brightly colored, carpeted library. It was stocked with books donated from many sources, but the most popular were happy little books supplied by the local dime-store manager. There were story hours in the library, and special reward times when a child went there to read or look at the pictures or just enjoy rolling on the soft rug.

Sister Marita used four rooms in the school building. Depending on how many volunteers she had on a given day, she directed some children in one room working on math problems while she taught a history lesson or a reading lesson in another, and had some children in the science room working on an experiment. The children were free to move from room to room as long as they went to another learning task and did not disturb others. Their options were determined by what

Sister had planned. In a sense, she ran an old "one-room" school although there were actually four rooms, and volunteers to give the children more freedom and more child-centered activities.

The children got many rewards. They were praised often for what they did. They marked their progress on charts and received a piece of candy when they had worked hard on a midafternoon lesson. Each had opportunities to perform by himself with a volunteer. Depending on the need that Sister Marita had identified, the tutor listened to a child read and asked him questions, read to him and let him retell the story, asked the child to dictate a story which became the "book" from which the child read, or played some game designed to give the child practice in word recognition or answering comprehension questions.

By giving the children more freedom, by showing them that the teacher expected them to learn, by treating them as individuals, and by praising them for their efforts and their successes, that one-woman school showed the children they could learn. That says a lot, because almost half the children who came to the school had failed at least one grade in their other school. The signs of success in Sister Marita's school were low absenteeism, and loyal parents who helped prepare lunches, beg money, and recruit other neighborhood children. Most of all, though, the results were in the happy faces of the children who wanted to read to you, show you the books they liked in the library, and tell you they enjoyed coming to school.

Programmed Tutoring. Very few people have the energy, nerve, and time to start their own school, even though many would like to have the freedom to develop their own curriculum and to help children as does Sister Marita. In sharp contrast to Sister Marita's project is a plan called programmed tutoring, so named because the words and actions of the tutor are closely controlled. A primary-grade child and tutor work to give the child needed practice in the lessons of his classroom book. The tutor has an instruction book to guide him in what he says and asks. The instructions match selections in the book. Basically, the tutor follows a teach-test pattern in getting the child to learn to pronounce words and to understand their meaning.

If the child pronounces the word correctly after one guided question, he continues to read. If the child fails a word, the tutor reads another set of directions to give a clearer understanding of the word and how it fits in the sentence. Then the child continues to read until he comes to another test word or to one he cannot pronounce.

The tutor needs only to hear the child read and to read to the child by following the manual. The tutor need not prepare lessons or materials. There is great ease in administering this program because the directions are prepared by a publishing company. The school needs only to identify which children will benefit and send them to the tutor. Usually the children who are having difficulty are sent twice a week. Programmed tutoring is limited to reading series that have been designed with accompanying tutor manuals.

The concept of programmed tutoring was developed by Dr. Douglas Ellson of Indiana University, and has been used by many school systems. The first major study of its effectiveness was in Indianapolis, where it was found to be significant in reducing transfers to special education classes. The study indicated that children in the bottom quarter of classes were moved into the next quarter after a year in programmed tutoring. Programmed tutoring is one of the few volunteer paid-aide programs evaluated through research. It showed the value of using laymen to help children learn to read.

Programmed tutoring seemed to work best with paid aides, because they often need this money to pay essential bills and are therefore unlikely to be absent. Children need regular and consistent practice in the early grades. With the paid worker and instructions in the manual, the child gets the benefit of regular and careful assistance at least twice a week. Other administrative considerations include identifying the children to receive the help, scheduling them and finding places for the sessions, and developing a reporting system for the tutor and teacher. A minimum-wage arrangement for tutors seemed to work well in most communities.

Thus, in two ways, programmed tutoring differs from the school of Sister Marita. Sister Marita created an alternative school for youngsters and encouraged tutors or volunteers to assist the children in a variety of ways. Both the children and volunteers had much freedom to explore. The programmed tutoring procedure attempted to support directly the skills being developed in the class, and the tutor followed a prescribed set of directions. Both worked well.

GENERAL ASSISTANCE PROGRAMS

WISE (Women in Service to Education). It's no wonder mothers with children in school look for ways to help elementary-school youngsters. Their instincts tell them that they ought to help others just as they would want their own child to be assisted if he ran into difficulty in learning. In Minneapolis, a large number of women's service groups have joined to form WISE (Women in Service to Education) as a means of giving reading aid to children in the elementary and junior high schools.

The participating organizations include the American Association of University Women, Association of Universalist Women, Church Women United of Minneapolis, Junior League of Minneapolis, League of Women Voters, Lutheran Social Service Auxiliary, Minneapolis Deanery of Catholic

Women, Minneapolis Section of the National Council of Jewish Women, Twin Cities Section of the National Council of Negro Women, Volunteer Service Bureau, and Woman's Club of Minneapolis.

In 1970, 822 WISE volunteers tutored in 67 elementary and junior high schools. They were recruited by the eleven women's organizations which had joined together to form WISE. Each member organization contributes ten dollars per year and two delegates to form a board of directors for WISE. The board advises member organizations of orientation dates, recruitment techniques, and makes suggestions to the coordinator of volunteer services, who is an employee of the Minneapolis public schools and whose office actually runs the program.

Recruitment is carried on within each of the eleven organizations by two delegates to the board. Various approaches are tried. Organizations such as the Council of Jewish Women and the American Association of University Women send a special annual mailing to all their members encouraging them to sign up for WISE. Other organizations such as the League of Women Voters include articles in their monthly newsletter asking for volunteer tutors; Church Women United sends fliers to the ministers of its member congregations and has had speakers from the WISE board talk at its area meetings.

The volunteer's time commitment is a minimum of two hours per week. During this time she works with three children, one after another for thirty to forty-five minutes each. She is briefed on the children's problems by their teacher, and because the volunteer works in the school, she has ready contact with the teacher. The intention is to forge a union between the teacher's knowledge and the volunteer's time to the benefit of the students. The WISE volunteer uses a written form to get instructions from the teacher.

After a volunteer applies to be a WISE tutor, she is invited to an orientation. She is assigned a school, and if she has a special request, it is honored. Each school then has its own briefing meeting. All volunteers are oriented to the school, and each meets her teacher, who outlines the needs of the children to help.

In addition to orientation, a volunteer receives a guidebook which contains suggestions on how she can be effective. She is invited to workshops for additional training and receives newsletters which contain helpful suggestions and information. The guidebook and newsletters are printed at the expense of the Minneapolis public schools.

Seattle, Washington—Children's Tutoring Service. The Seattle Children's Tutoring Service began in 1958 with six volunteer women from the National Council of Jewish Women. The program has grown steadily. In 1966 there were 199 volunteer tutors helping about 200 children in 50 of the 86 Seattle public schools.

The women served as reading tutors for children in the elementary grades. Each had taken a course in reading improvement from an instructor in the Seattle schools. Classes consisting of four two-hour sessions were given whenever the number of volunteers warranted them. The instructor also acted as a liaison between the schools and the Council of Jewish Women. Upon completion of the course, each volunteer was assigned to assist a pupil in a nearby school once a week for about an hour. Many women helped more than one child, and some tutored two or three times weekly. The instructor visited each tutor and observed her work. The salary of the instructor was $125 a month for the nine school months.

In 1967 the Seattle public schools assumed costs and responsibilities of the program. Since then various women's organizations have provided volunteers and have maintained a council member on the Tutoring Advisory Board. Volunteers have worked as reading and arithmetic tutors, classroom helpers, kindergarten and book-club aides, helping with book selection and reading. They have served in the primary enrichment program, reading to children; instructed fifth and sixth grades in dance, art, oceanography, etc.; coached in the children's theater; helped make puppets; and maintained a talent bank, providing a person talented in music or art on special occasions.

These activities are now served by the Council of Jewish Women, Parent-Teacher Association, B'nai B'rith, Council of Negro Women, Junior League of Seattle, and the Associated Students (University of Washington and Seattle Pacific College).

During the 1968–1969 school year, 1,585 volunteers served regularly during an average week. Of these, 1,135 were in elementary schools and 450 in junior and senior high schools. These volunteers participated two or more hours each week. Another 1,250 tutored weekly at Neighborhood House Tutorial Centers and at St. Peter Claver Interracial Center. Special training was provided for recruits interested in helping non-English-speaking children.

With new developments in the program, such as the Community Resource Bureau, the variety of services, and the increase of volunteers in secondary schools, the Seattle group felt it was important to have someone on the school staff to coordinate the program. Teachers must be informed about what is available; schedules must be worked out; volunteers need to be given orientation and to be shown where to work and where they may secure materials. These and other chores are the responsibility of the staff coordinator. He may be a counselor, an administrative assistant, an instructional assistant, or, if necessary, the principal. Whoever the coordinator is, he must believe in the potential of the volunteer program and must have adequate time for the program.

It is clear that volunteers can and will offer many hours of service if given the chance by the school system. Seattle's experience points out, however, that training and coordination are indispensable to success. When it comes to reading, it should be kept in mind that the child needs practice several times a week. Thus, volunteers in reading should be free to work with the child a minimum of twice a week. The probability for success is much greater when the child has frequent, short practice sessions instead of one long session a week.

The Seattle experience shows that the social and service clubs of a large city can provide immense human resources for a large school system if the system is willing to take on the role of coordinating the volunteer activities.

Public Schools Take Leadership. Volunteer efforts have made considerable impact on public schools. Many cities—Los Angeles, Indianapolis, Cleveland, Cincinnati, and others—have assigned coordination of volunteer efforts to a full-time staff member. Cincinnati is a case in point. Like most large cities, it has many children who cannot read well. The public school system made two key decisions: it would concentrate on the poor reader in poverty neighborhoods and make extensive use of volunteers.

To have an idea of what to do, Cincinnati first tried to get a picture of the needs of these readers and their problems. Attempts to summarize difficulties of children in school are unsatisfactory because no description of their problem and its origin is typical of all. These children are not typed, but have differences in achievement, social and personal adjustment, interest, and attitudes. Their retardation in school subjects stems from many factors.

It was found that many of the Cincinnati children came from homes where there was a lack of understanding of modern urban living as well as educational and cultural handicaps arising from backgrounds of deprivation. The home environment included family patterns of divorce, unemployment, sickness, retardation, or delinquency. There was no motivation or confidence in the family members' ability to improve their situation. Frequent moves, caused by inability to function in a largely automated urban environment, and withdrawal from competition were common. Most homes lacked books and newspapers.

The children in need of reading help often exhibited a short attention span, little imagination, difficulty with unfamiliar items on a test, lack of ambition, and insufficient reading skills.

To counteract these problems, the Cincinnati schools decided to provide a tutorial program using volunteers. School personnel anticipated that a one-to-one relationship of pupil to tutor would help the students learn the subject matter. A study found that many educationally disadvantaged pupils are less able to learn from conventional classroom instruction than their more advantaged peers. As these pupils fall behind, their problems become compounded, and soon they find themselves feeling lost and abandoned. In addition to facing learning problems, these pupils often are absent from school, which sets them behind even further. Individual instruction is a major solution, but it can be implemented only with additional adult help.

Cincinnati decided it had an even more important goal— to develop a personal-social relationship between pupil and tutor. It was assumed the attention and interest of the tutor toward the elementary pupil would lift the pupil's aspiration level and self-esteem and make him a more productive, more motivated person. In addition, the tutor's example of correct, clear, courteous speech; promptness in keeping appointments; and a serious attitude toward responsibilities and privileges shared with the pupil were expected to increase the pupil's efficiency and chance for success in school.

Cincinnati also felt it should make available to these problem readers a pleasant, quiet place to study where resource materials were accessible. With these objectives in mind, the Cincinnati schools developed their program.

The first school-wide effort to initiate the program began

in the summer of 1964 when a group of women, interested in tutoring pupils with reading problems, met with the Board of Education and agreed to supply volunteer tutors in the elementary schools during the school day. This group was called Volunteers in Public Schools (VIPS) and presently comprises representatives from the Women's City Club, the Junior League of Cincinnati, the Cincinnati Elementary School Council of PTA's, Cincinnati Section of the Council of Jewish Women, the Unitarian-Universalist Council, the Inner-Parish Women, and the Sisterhood of the Isaac M. Wise Temple.

The purpose of VIPS was to supply volunteers to tutor on a one-to-one basis, work in remedial reading programs, and work in cultural enrichment programs. In the second year the Cincinnati public schools expanded the in-school sessions to include twenty-six elementary and six junior-high study centers. Additional centers were established in October, 1965, as a result of further funding from the Office of Economic Opportunity. Centers were located in forty elementary schools and seven junior high schools. The program was funded in 1967 under the Disadvantaged Pupils Public Fund (DPPF), a bill passed by the Ohio state legislature.

Tutoring centers are in schools where there is a concentration of educationally disadvantaged youth. Each center is supervised by a professional teacher or an administrative aide. It is the professional teacher's job to schedule pupils with tutors, act as liaison between school and tutor, and help tutors to achieve their goals. Elementary-school centers are open from three-thirty to five P.M., Tuesday through Thursday, to encourage children to study on their own and to spend additional time with their tutor.

Tutors are recruited through the many women's clubs and organizations already mentioned. The major qualification is that they are warm, interested persons who enjoy being with and helping young school-age children. An adult tutor is required to have a high-school certificate or sufficient experience in a comparable educational program and a reference. A high-school pupil who wants to tutor must be recommended by his counselor, and parental permission must be obtained before an assignment is made. A college student may volunteer, and can satisfy some college requirements through the program.

In order to serve in the elementary-school centers, tutors must be available at least one day a week (Tuesday, Wednesday, Thursday) from three-thirty to five P.M. Tutors must serve once or twice each week for at least one semester.

Each center's director is available to arrange schedules and to guide tutors on teaching methods and content. In addition, tutors may receive in-service training from the coordinators of the program. The pupil's teacher informs the tutor of the pupil's difficulties.

Leadership comes from the supervisor of Tutorial and Volunteer Services and the director of elementary schools, who is involved in all phases of the Tutorial-Study Center Program and responsible for operational decisions. There are also a supervisor and a coordinator. The principal in each school assigns tutorial stations and study rooms, and contacts parents of children being tutored to explain the purpose of the program and let them know when it starts. He also promotes all phases of the program. The director of program development, who was instrumental in establishing the program, continues to serve in an advisory capacity.

The power of the Cincinnati program lies in the organizational and financial support of the school system. Volunteers have supervision and a room or center to work in. They can concentrate their efforts on the child and not on organization. The status and continuity of the tutorial program are maintained by the school.

New Orleans Tutoring Program. In New Orleans the local chapter of the National Council of Jewish Women agreed to work with second- and fifth-grade students in a project using programmed instruction. This program provides reading instruction in short steps and gives problems that can be solved using recently learned skills. The text gives the correct answer so the children know whether to proceed or ask for help. Materials are easy for the volunteer to use because specialized training is not required. The New Orleans Volunteer Tutoring Project worked on the theory that pupils doing poorly in reading can profit by slow, step-by-step instruction. The volunteers also felt that the one-to-one approach gave a slow-moving child the encouragement and pacing needed for success. The Council of Jewish Women agreed with one school that each volunteer would take three fifth-graders and six second-graders as far as she could through the twelve books in the programmed series in the Behavioral Research Lab's Program over a two-year period.

Orientation and training included a half-day training session in the beginning of the year to show the volunteers how to use the material, and a monthly meeting or telephone conversation with each volunteer concerning the children's progress and their problems. Discussions with the teachers and the principal were held every two months, and there was an evaluation meeting in March.

The estimated cost of books and training for a volunteer, three fifth-graders, and six second-graders is $100 a year. Evaluation showed progress of fifth-graders to be minimal and the problems difficult. They needed more variety. Second-graders, on the other hand, seemed to progress very satisfactorily and to enjoy the material.

On this basis, it was decided to help only second-graders in terms of the program.

Communities Organize: Saginaw, Michigan. Most communities now have an organization that promotes community action on problems. Education is certainly a community problem. If a reading volunteer group does not function as part of the Community Action Program in your neighborhood, why not form one? Here is a sample of what one community did when it recognized a need to help its youth become better readers.

After a teen-ager was fatally stabbed by a gang on July 4, 1966, in Saginaw, Michigan, a group of mothers met to discuss the problem and to seek a means of deterring future tragedies. This group was eventually joined by several local PTA groups.

At a subsequent public meeting an opinion was formed that most crimes by young people were closely related to the school dropout. The dropout, in turn, was identified as a problem reader. Thus, it appeared that one approach to the problem was an effort to aid the poor reader in his early days of school. RE-AD was begun.

RE-AD represents Reading Advice, or Reading Adventure —depending on the volunteer, who spends one hour or more each week acting as a "friend to youths." Their sessions are oriented toward learning skills or directed toward building a friendly relationship. Eleventh- and twelfth-graders, college students, adults with a variety of backgrounds, and Senior Citizens form the RE-AD corps of volunteers.

RE-AD creates close ties between a youngster and an older person, similar to the Big Brother program. Guidance and educational opportunity go hand in hand.

More than two hundred volunteers were organized to work with children in the late afternoon or early evening. The primary emphasis was on motivating the youngster to appreciate the value of reading. They were assigned to one of many churches or community groups cooperating in the program. Each tutor worked with one child at a time. The activities at each center—programming, tutor guidance, and logistics— were guided by a supervisor.

The supervisors were teachers or professional people.

They saw that the physical setting was ready and advised the tutors, which kept things going smoothly. Most supervisors spent two to three hours a week at this job, which involved phone calls, organizing materials, showing new ideas, and being available during the meeting hour.

A local distributor of paperbacks and school materials donated hundreds of dollars' worth of books to the project. These included easy readers, phonics and reading work books, and paperback read-aloud stories and biographies. Each center furnished its own glue, crayons, construction paper, or other needed materials. RE-AD prepares a kit of word games each year to replenish ideas in each center. Volunteers were encouraged to use the backs of cereal boxes for flash cards and puzzles, because they are the sort of things the child can take home or can duplicate with materials around the house.

On the basis of favorable tutor reaction, RE-AD directors feel the program has been successful. Enthusiasm for the project is expressed in these lines from an editorial in the Saginaw News: "It seems that the RE-AD idea could be applied on a nationwide basis. In fact, the situation is ripe for a recommendation to be made in the right places in Washington."

A program that intends to motivate and create an atmosphere of friendship relies heavily on the abilities of the volunteers. RE-AD has protected itself by having supervisors at each site. The supervisors have experience in dealing with people and in motivating young children to learn. The other ingredient in RE-AD that makes for success is the volunteers' use of materials common to most households. Cereal boxes, newspapers, paperback books, and so on are used. In this way, the child begins to see that reading can be useful in daily life and that there are always opportunities to practice. Utility and ease of practice are characteristic of the kinds of things that appeal to the potential dropout.

Racine, Wisconsin—Reading Listeners. Sometimes a community's needs are so diverse that groups want to help in a variety of activities related to reading. Two groups of women in Racine, Wisconsin, identified several language, reading, and motivational needs they thought volunteers could help with—in the schools, in libraries, and on field trips.

Communication within the elementary classroom often depends on the children having some common experiences. Whether through discussion, reading, or writing, communication must start with a common base. Volunteers can often provide these common experiences, enabling the teacher and the children to build on them for instructional purposes.

During 1963–1964 the Racine branch of the American Association of University Women and the YWCA studied the needs of disadvantaged children in Racine. The study showed a need for more *reading help*, more social experiences, more field trips, and more preschools.

In the spring of 1964 a service was set up to recruit five volunteer reading listeners to work in one of the inner-city schools. This service expanded each year until it served eight inner-city elementary schools and three junior high schools, and recruited about 150 volunteer reading listeners. Each volunteer spends a half-day or more a week in school and works under the teacher's direction. Children who need extra help with reading are given a chance to work on a one-to-one basis for about twenty or thirty minutes.

Recruiting was done carefully. AAUW and YWCA members and reading listeners already in the schools told friends, relatives, and neighbors that the program needed men and women, ages eighteen to eighty, who liked children and who were patient with them. Recruiters explained that no special training was necessary because reading listeners were *not teaching*. Recruiters sent names of interested people to the Recruitment Committee chairman, who interviewed the volunteer and made the school placement. The work of the committee ended with recruitment and school placement.

Teachers reported the program improved the child's self-concept to such an extent that the *reading help was secondary*. Reading listeners often said, "This is the most satisfying volunteer work I have done in my life. I have never felt so needed." They conveyed this feeling to their friends and acquainted Racine people with the tremendous need for enriching the lives of the disadvantaged child, the potential dropout. Speakers from the program were available to clubs and organizations.

About fifty-five children at a time attended festive parties in the Garden Room at the YWCA. Ten to thirteen parties were given each year. The majority were financed by the Kiwanis Club, with services recruited by AAUW. Others were financed, serviced, or both by churches, Jaycettes, AAUW, and the Women's Club. Approximately 4,000 children have attended parties.

A request for neighborhood book service from the Breakthrough Neighborhood Center brought an offer of a small house owned by the city. Collaboration began with Racine Public Library, the Johnson Foundation, Neighborhood Youth Corps, and Western Publishing. Book circulation, story hours, book-report contests, games, and reading-centered handicrafts were organized. A supervisor from the neighborhood was paid by the Johnson Foundation, and AAUW and the YWCA provided five volunteers.

The center provides a home atmosphere for book browsing and borrowing, reading, story hours, crafts, and educational games. Located in one of the city's inner-core areas, its purpose is bringing children and books together in the hope of starting reading habits that will assist in future schooling and employment. The library provides approximately seven hundred children's books formerly from the Classroom Libraries collection.

The Public Affairs Committee of the YWCA and the Community Problems Committee of the American Association of University Women were approached by the Education

Committee of Project Breakthrough with a proposal to start some kind of reading program at the center. The committee chairman, in turn, approached the library for funds; instead, the library offered books, and with board approval, was able to pay the Book House staff salaries (a director, an assistant, and two neighborhood Youth Corps summer workers) when other funding sources were not available.

The city librarian is responsible for final administrative decisions. The Book House Steering Committee meets bimonthly to discuss and evaluate the program. Members of the committee represent the community agencies.

In one six-month operation, over 4,000 children visited the Book House. Some 1,300 books circulated in addition to those read on the premises, and a federal grant for salaries with which to continue the work of this community "mini-library" was received.

The Racine design also included a unit of the Reading is Fun-damental gift-book distribution project, patterned after a program in Washington, D.C. Gifts of books and bookshelves were made in federally funded after-school study centers and in two regular classrooms. Books and bookshelves were earned by the class as awards.

Another element was the "Hooked on Books" project developed by Daniel Fader, which also called for free distribution of paperback books and magazines. Two volunteers worked in this project.

The diversity in the Racine project does not necessarily mean confusion. Racine is able to manage its diversity by keeping in mind its central purpose: providing additional experiences to the child that will assist him in learning to read and in wanting to read.

Birmingham: Reading Disability and Cultural Enrichment Program. Ordinarily, educational specialists discourage laymen from trying to remedy severe reading problems because of their complexity. There are some attempts, however, to make use of volunteers to work with children who have severe reading problems. The University of Alabama Medical School uses volunteers to help learners through a specific set of exercises developed by James Shedd, director of the school's Reading Disabilities Clinic. The Junior League and the Council of Jewish Women provide volunteers and communication with the community.

Volunteers work with children who have been examined by professional diagnosticians. A test program was run with fifty-one children from nine o'clock until noon every Saturday for nine weeks. The volunteers used the materials developed by Dr. Shedd, and the children in the program made significant gains on a standardized reading test.

This program shows that laymen can help in remedial cases as long as there is sufficient preparation and the work is precisely defined. Just as in programmed tutoring, the volunteers were prepared by several hours of orientation (five in the Birmingham program), and they were taught to use materials that did not ask for diagnosis by them. The volunteer was, in a sense, carrying out a prescription prepared by the professional diagnostician.

The service of the Disabilities Clinic was expanded into the public schools after the pilot program was completed. Kindergarten teachers were given a fifteen-hour workshop to teach them to recognize specific symptoms. They were to refer children needing help from clinic personnel and in classes taught by volunteers using special materials. The materials carry the student through a sequence of phonics and writing exercises designed to imprint visual images on his mind.

The Junior League of Birmingham and the National Council of Jewish Women obtained volunteers, arranged for training, established schedules, and supervised participation. The Parent-Teacher Association in schools served by the program provided a chairman who aided in recruiting and coordinating volunteers.

A six-hour workshop (three hours a day for two days) was held in September for the volunteers. Each received a teacher's and student's manual as well as other materials used in the program. The teacher's manual outlined each program plan in great detail, thereby permitting a volunteer to effectively use the materials. Use of these materials was thoroughly discussed at this workshop and others conducted throughout the school year.

According to an evaluation questionnaire, the program was well accepted by teachers, principals, and superintendent.

In 1969 the Birmingham section, National Council of Jewish Women, initiated a cultural-enrichment program for third-graders under the auspices of the Guidance Department of the Birmingham Board of Education.

Volunteers read stories to each third-grade class from the Random House series of books. Each book dealt with a certain concept, i.e., behavior, respect, courage. Then, using prepared questions, the class was encouraged to discuss the stories they had just heard. These stories stimulated conversation and responses from the children which hopefully would carry over to their other schoolwork.

An orientation for volunteers was conducted by the head of the Guidance Department. A second session was an actual classroom demonstration conducted by a guidance counselor. Volunteers served ten Birmingham schools once a week for two six-week periods. An hour was spent in each class. The classroom teacher remained in the room. Once assigned to a school, the volunteer came under the supervision of the guidance counselor of that school.

One volunteer found that attendance increased on the day she was there.

Fall River: Books Exposure Program. Many children find

it difficult to experience an adult-to-child contact in the school, although they often want and need someone to relate to. The Books Exposure Program fills these needs. The volunteer who helps a child interact more positively with the real world and to the world of books shows the child that an adult is interested in him and will spend time with him.

The Books Exposure Program of Fall River was geared toward children who are economically as well as educationally disadvantaged. Sponsored initially by the Council for Public Schools, Boston, which was later joined by the National Book Committee, the basic purposes of the program were to develop positive pupil attitudes toward reading at home, reading in the school, owning books, and visiting libraries. If these children could be motivated to like reading, it was hoped they would become better students. If the child feels no need to read, he does not improve, and the skills taught in school never develop simply because they're not used. The Books Exposure Program proposed to make the child want to read by giving him security with books, helping him like them, and promoting a need to read.

The Books Exposure Program was also aimed at the parents of disadvantaged children. In the studies conducted in Fall River it was found that the educationally and economically deprived parents do not necessarily lack interest in school or in the child's involvement there. Most of their contacts with schools have been negative. Teachers have called them because the child is failing, is causing problems to the school, or is having problems adjusting.

The Books Exposure Program created a different atmosphere. An attempt was made to keep parents informed, and convincing evidence was found that parents' attitudes and relationships with the school were positively affected.

The core of the program was a weekly session in which a volunteer met with ten children in the school. The volunteer's main purpose was to get the children interested in books. Each week a particular book—one considered good children's literature by both authorities and the children themselves—was featured. The volunteer used a handbook for suggested activities or was free to use his own ideas. They acted out scenes, wrote poems or reactions, played games, made costumes, taped plays, and performed similar activities. Volunteers agreed that they were highly successful in inspiring children to read for pleasure.

Because most of these children lacked verbal skills, they were encouraged to express themselves. Volunteers were prompted to praise children's original written work or oral expression. Many of the children's written efforts were photocopied and made into booklets which were mailed to each child who contributed. The volunteers reported that the children were "greatly impressed and pleased by this material evidence of the worth of their efforts."

A second segment of the program was the Gift Book Selection. Four times a year children could choose a book to keep for their own. A preprogram survey conducted in 1968 showed that more than half of these children had no children's books in their homes. It was difficult, therefore, for them to grasp that they could keep the books, take them home, and read them as often as they liked. The choice was made from a display of thirty or more books. The Books Exposure staff observed a change in the children's behavior from the first gift-book selection to the end of the program. Children began to devote more time before making a decision on one they wanted to keep. Some children even tried to read an entire book before making it their final selection.

A third segment of the Books Exposure Program aimed at changing the child's feeling about a library. Parents of the project children did not often take them to the library, so a library visit was made. The children's responses were enthusiastic. Some expressed a desire to return and said they would ask their parents to take them.

The Fall River school system was responsible for daily administration of the program, though it was directed and supervised by Dr. Gertrude Bullen. A Fall River administrator familiar with the school personnel and the organization coordinated the program. Local school personnel were involved in the individual schools—including selecting grades and teachers and the facilities. Successful volunteers included housewives, former teachers, college students, mothers who wanted to become teacher aides, a librarian, retired businessmen, a hairdresser, a waitress, and a school custodian who wanted to find out "whether the program could really work."

Teachers were involved to the degree that they wanted. Some left the program entirely to the volunteers, while others actively participated. Four orientation sessions were required of the volunteers. At these sessions, aims of the program, its organization, and responsibilities of the teachers and volunteers were explained. The program was funded in the first year by the National Endowment for the Humanities. During the second year the public school administrators were convinced of its value and agreed to support the cost of the books as well as donate administrative time to the program. In its third year, interested citizens, civic groups, teachers' associations, industries, and the Roman Catholic archdiocese contributed five thousand dollars to the program. The Ford Foundation supported almost half of the program's expense during the third year.

The Books Exposure Program was established with a preconceived evaluation plan to determine its effectiveness. Dr. Bullen measured the attitudes of children, parents, volunteers, and teachers. She found there were significant positive changes in the attitudes of the children toward reading, books, and libraries. They read more, too. Similar positive gains were made in the attitudes of the parents. They saw the school contributing more to their child and were more willing to work with the school as a result.

The technical aspects of the attitude measures and of the research techniques may be of interest to administrators of programs. A summary of the study can be obtained from the National Book Committee, One Park Avenue, New York, New York 10016. This committee also has information on the Books Exposure activities for those who want more detailed information on how the volunteers and children accomplished the positive attitudes. More of this kind of evaluation is needed to help us decide on volunteer programs that significantly change the reading performance of children.

LIBRARY PROGRAMS

More and more public libraries are focusing their resources on out-reach programs, especially services to the disadvantaged. In these, the library becomes the fulcrum for two kinds of service —making books and other media directly accessible to readers and potential readers in all age groups, often in new, unconventional ways; and indirectly providing materials and all kinds of help to adults working with children, training them in the art of storytelling, to take a simple example.

In cities as disparate as Sacramento, California, and Brooklyn, New York, and in many communities, libraries have transported books into neighborhoods. The Pied Piper summer program in Sacramento has been operated jointly by the City-County Library and the YWCA. A van cruised the northwestern section of the city, stopping whenever clusters of children were found. Brooklyn's similar, inner-city safaris have been documented in an appealing and sensitive short film called *Who Grows in Brooklyn*, available through Carousel Films in New York.

Among many other programs of indirect service, the

Reading, Pennsylvania, Public Library has cooperated by supplying books and other materials, and advice, to the seven-
church Southwest Christian Ministry which offers reading
enrichment to students in grades one through four, with thirty
volunteers participating; to Kennedy House, a Roman Catholic
study and tutoring center; and to the principal of a grade school
in a predominantly black area who asked white Methodist
church members to volunteer an hour a week to help first-grade
boys and girls. Twenty volunteers have worked for two years
by talking and reading to the children, listening to them as they
learned to read, helping them with math, and just talking about
things they were learning in school.

An inventory of programs like these can be found later in
this book as Appendix A.

READING IS FUN-DAMENTAL

Another kind of approach can be seen in the growth of the
coordinated national effort launched several years ago by a
group of women in Washington, D.C., who were shocked by
conditions in the capital's schools, and who decided to act.
From this concern came: Reading is Fun-damental.

Find ways of getting books to the kids, and they will read.
That has been the assumption animating a group headed by
Mrs. Robert McNamara, wife of the former Secretary of Defense. Working with libraries and other community agencies
as private citizens, they have especially attempted to get books
to children and adults in poverty areas. They emphasized that
reading is *fun*, with the hope that their attitude and the books
they provide would encourage children to want to continue
reading. The other theme that the group promoted is that reading is a basic ingredient to success. Thus their slogan and organization title, "Reading is Fun-damental" (RIF).

RIF began in Washington, D.C., in 1966. D.C. Citizens for

Better Public Education sponsored a pilot project, backed by several foundation grants and enthusiastic volunteers. The purpose of RIF was to motivate the inner-city child to read by giving him inexpensive paperback books to keep. The child chose a book on the basis of its special appeal to him—a choice unhampered by adult standards. Because the child owned the book, he could take it home, lend it to a friend, or share it with others. The primary target was school-age children, but the program tried to relate to the larger community by making books available to teen-agers, adults, and preschoolers.

To stimulate interest and enjoyment in reading, Reading is Fun-damental focused on two techniques: self-selection and ownership of books. RIF firmly believed that children feel strongly about choosing their own books and that encouraging a disadvantaged child to choose, using his own standards, would help him to realize his own self-worth and to know that he is appreciated as an individual. Many disadvantaged children know only too well the stigma of hand-me-down possessions. RIF felt that they would respond enthusiastically to ownership of an attractive new book.

RIF leaves the responsibility of providing funds for books to the local community, though it can provide some funds for guidance and administration. In Washington, RIF employed a community worker to operate a bookmobile in the inner city. Federal City College contributed the services of another young man. Community volunteers helped by distributing books and keeping records. The City College worker gathered groups of children and teen-agers, talked to them, read to them, and listened to them read. Reading is Fun-damental workers encouraged the children to come back the week after they had read their books to tell about the story. The children were always encouraged to go to the library, and many children and adults got library cards. One visible result was better relations between the library and the community.

RIF also cooperated with the Capitol East Community

Organization in stimulating library use through an incentive program. For every twelve books a student signed out of the library, he was permitted to select a RIF book to keep for his own. Three branch libraries in an adjacent community, responding to pressure from schoolchildren in their area who learned about the program, requested RIF books so they, too, could participate.

Reading is Fun-damental has cooperated with many organizations—public schools, Church Women United, the Roman Catholic Church, Neighborhood Youth Corps, the Women's Board of Children's Hospital, and Seventh-Day Adventists. In its effort to get children to read and take pride in books, it has sponsored such activities as a Black Art and Book Fair, a tutorial program in communication skills, and a story-reading and storytelling hour.

RIF has extended its operation from Washington to large cities like Cleveland, Ohio, Pittsburgh, Pennsylvania, and to smaller cities like Huntington, West Virginia, and Flagstaff, Arizona. Programs have been implemented to reach inner-city black children, Hopi and Navajo children, white Appalachian children, and Mexican-American children.

The operating moneys of the national office of the Reading is Fun-damental are for general guidance and for setting up model programs. The model projects are adapted to local needs, and the responsibility for financing resides with the community.

Simply supplying books, however, does not make readers. That's why tutorial services, storytellers, and practice reading sessions are often built into RIF programs. The effort at Flagstaff indicates the care that is taken to make a book distribution program work.

Books for Indians. The Teacher Corps in Flagstaff started a Reading is Fun-damental program in response to an invitation from the national RIF office. This was an attempt to reach

4,500 Navajo and Hopi Indian children in five areas around Flagstaff.

The first distribution of books was in the schools; however, because so many teachers led the children in the choice of books, RIF decided the program didn't belong in the schools. Selected sites were then visited once a month by an Avis-donated bookmobile. The children received an average of six books each, the books provided by $7,500 seed money from the National Home Library Foundation. "Unfortunately, many times local people get the impression that foundations will provide funds indefinitely—for years and years," commented Charles Supplee, Flagstaff director. "In some cases, they lose interest when they find out they'll have to raise their own money." This was particularly a problem among the Indians, whose median income is $1,300 a year.

To encourage them, RIF promised to donate the bookmobile to the tribes being served if they guaranteed $10,000 or more to the program for the next three years.

Evidence that RIF is having an effect on the Hopi and Navajo children came from comments of several area principals. They reported that reading levels at their schools had gone up noticeably, especially where teachers use the RIF books for supplemental reading.

The Navajo and Hopi reservations cover an area of more than 127,000 square miles, approximately the size of West Virginia. Communities are small, isolated, and widely separated and may consist of a trading post and a cluster of hogans (Navajo homes); a large boarding school; a mission; a chapter house; or pueblo villages of the Hopi. The Navajo population is about 120,000, the largest Indian tribe in the nation; the Hopi population is about 6,000. Although these figures may be small compared to other minority groups, the isolated conditions under which the majority of the people live merits a concentrated effort to make this program succeed.

Public library facilities may be as far away as 200 miles—the average being 75 miles from a community. There are libraries, for example, in Gallup, New Mexico, and in Flagstaff, Arizona. Unlike city children, Navajo children have little access to books. The lack of reading material during the summer often results in serious educational regression by the fall. A method of book distribution through the summer greatly supports the total educational program of the children. Thus, Indian children are a specific program target for RIF.

The first step in choosing books for distribution in the Flagstaff area was to determine the basic interests of the recipients. This was established by a Suggestion Committee made up of Teacher Corps interns, teachers, and cooperating librarians in several schools scattered throughout the Navajo and Hopi reservations. Information was also collected on which books children took from school libraries.

The second step was asking publishers for samples in the areas and grade levels determined by the Suggestion Committee. Because there was no "publishers' list of books for Indian children," this solicitation was a crucial step. Books chosen for purchase and subsequent distribution were listed by the Selection Committee.

Final selection of books to purchase was accomplished by displaying the sample books to about 2,000 Hopi and Navajo children, primarily through the junior high schools, and asking each of them to choose five books they would like to have. The combined results determined the titles, which Navajo-Hopi RIF purchased.

Five areas on the Navajo and Hopi reservations were chosen to participate in the pilot RIF program. These areas were in or around schools and communities in which Navajo-Hopi Teacher Corps teams were established so that parents and interested citizens could be guided by them.

Distribution was on a scheduled basis. During the year, distribution in the boarding schools took place in the dormitories, which were the children's home for nine months. Scheduled reading times aided RIF in developing the desire to read through self-selection and then ownership. The children were encouraged to trade books with roommates.

Books were also distributed in chapter houses (public meeting places), trading posts, and other gathering places. Upper-level books for adults were distributed through basic-adult-education classes conducted by Teacher Corps teams on the reservations.

Approximately 4,000 children were in the schools and areas comprising this pilot program. Allowing four or five books per child during the initial distribution, between 15,000 and 20,000 books were purchased for school-year distribution. Summer distributions required double this number.

Funds were solicited through IMAGE, a nonprofit corporation engaging in and promoting projects and studies dealing with intercultural education designed to develop self-determination and self-image. Projected cost of the pilot program was established at between $35,000 and $70,000. This included books, coordination, vehicle, mileage, office and research materials, and miscellaneous expenses.

The List of Books. Because a free book distribution is expensive, a local RIF group must make sure that its books match the interests of the children to be served. The Flagstaff selection procedure makes the choices fairly valid for the age group involved. A similar procedure in the Cleveland project produced a booklist of 400 titles.

The Cleveland group found that most youngsters tend to choose colorful books with attractive pictures. Books with comic characters, such as *Charlie Brown*, *Dennis the Menace* (both Fawcett Crest series), and *Marmaduke* (Scholastic series) have been popular at all age levels. Interestingly, books of an instructional nature, such as *How to Care for Your Dog* and *Sewing Is Fun* (Scholastic) have also been in great demand.

Books about animals seem to have a special appeal to primary-grade children. The Golden Press Shape Books have been popular with this group.

The *How and Why Science Series* (Grosset and Dunlap) and biographies, such as *She Wanted to Read: The Story of Mary McLeod Bethune* and *The Story of Phillis Wheatley* (Archway), have been very much in demand by intermediate-grade children. Also, those books which have a familiar face on the cover, as does *Cool Cos: The Story of Bill Cosby* (Scholastic), have been especially appealing.

RIF recognizes that it must revise its booklist continually to meet the needs of the children. For example, there is a great need for more books dealing with the lives and experience of non-middle-class and nonwhite children. Publishers of children's books should increase the number of books concerning blacks in the picture-book and primary-grade reading levels, and the number of books concerning American Indian, Chinese, Japanese, and Spanish-American teen-agers in upper-grade reading levels.

RIF in Appalachia. The Reading is Fun-damental program based in Huntington, West Virginia, is an Appalachian pilot project under the national RIF program. Some 2,000 children in Lincoln, Mingo, and Wayne counties and the city of Huntington have received nearly 10,000 books in the last two years.

In an interview, Miss Jeanne Young, coordinator, described the program in each area: Lincoln County, one of the ten poorest counties in the United States, is "very rural." Low-income residents, mostly parents, served as distributors of the books in three schools and the county parent-child center. In Mingo County RIF operated mainly through Head Start centers and schools.

Wayne County's people are antagonistic to the schools, so it was more difficult to set up a RIF project there. Transportation posed another problem, for only 500 of the 3,000 population live in town; the rest are scattered in hard-to-reach areas.

However, Avis donated a bookmobile, and two volunteers from Marshall College in Huntington helped distribute books.

In Huntington, the PTA raised some money, and Teacher Corps interns set up an after-school program to help the children read the books they had received from RIF.

One teacher told Miss Young that she thought the RIF program has been more helpful than her county's remedial reading program, because (1) the children choose the books they want to read and get to take them home and read them as many times as they want; (2) the parents are reading with the children—many for the first time; and (3) a child will tackle a tough book and read as much as he can because he really wants to read that particular book.

4 ❧ Thirteen-Plus Programs

THE MORE successful programs offering young adults and older persons a chance to acquire or improve reading skills and habits show, in general, the common principle of practicality —a demonstration of how reading relates directly to the achievement of important immediate goals: staying in school, getting or holding a job. Thus reading is taught and practiced in a larger motivational context, such as the "school without walls" Parkway Project in Philadelphia; the Drop-in School in Des Moines, Iowa; the learning center in Long Beach, California, which was set up for students excluded from regular school because of drug abuse; the Upward Bound programs in various parts of the country; Urban League Street Academies in several cities; and VISTA volunteer schools.

Other programs described here focus more directly on literacy training for adults and young people, where motivational influences and factors are combined with easy access to the books and other materials which sustain the development of reading habits. Still others reflect routine and unusual extensions of library service to persons who are, for reasons of health or institutional confinement, denied ready access to the books they need and want.

PHILADELPHIA PARKWAY PROJECT

Change can come from within the educational structure as well as from without. Philadelphia's Parkway Project uses the community as its classroom and teaches a variety of skills through trips to the newspaper and the library, through billboards, and through work experience in local shops and businesses.

The project, popularly known as the "school without walls," opened in February, 1969. There is no school building as such. Instead, classes meet in the Philadelphia Museum of Art, City Hall, as well as the Museum of Natural History, insurance and telephone offices, newspaper plants, Franklin Institute, churches, and similar places.

Staffing and curriculum are unusual. A corps of certified teachers is augmented by full-time college-student interns and part-time community assistants. Each team conducts tutorial groups of fifteen students, teaching subjects ranging from French and spelling to art and candlemaking.

About half of the 250 courses offered are led by community professionals, skilled craftsmen, businessmen, and parents, who contribute their time and expertise. These volunteers range from company executives and natural scientists in whose offices and institutions classes are held to such entrepreneurs as a photographer, a master auto mechanic, and an architect, who teach their own specialties.

After requirements in English, history, math, and science have been met, students are free to take what they want, virtually anywhere they want. Because classes are extremely small (some consisting of two or three students), mobility is seldom a problem.

The director of the Parkway Project, John Bremer, took two years to develop his staff. He drew on the community and asked volunteers to convey to the students the excitement they found in their professions.

It is still too early to know whether this unorthodox approach to education will work. Philadelphia students seem to want it. One hundred and fifty started in the program. Ten thousand applied for the 500 seats available in 1970. Officials had to resort to a goldfish-bowl lottery as a fair method of selecting participants.

DES MOINES DROP-IN SCHOOL

Des Moines, Iowa, shows another way that a school system can adapt its operation to a specific educational problem, the school dropout—establish a "drop-in" school for dropouts.

Bright colors transform the walls and doors of the school's warehouse into a mood for the young generation. Two floor-to-ceiling murals display silhouettes of bell-bottom-trousered, guitar-carrying moderns. The men who built the structure thought they had installed overhead roll-up doors. The Drop-In staff sees the doors (with windows painted in) as a means to display twenty-foot murals. There are no interior walls. Instead, six-foot bookshelves and blackboard dividers create comfortable work areas for art, English, coffee and Coke drinking, supply buying, basic math instruction, office-skills practice, and science lessons.

The work areas are occupied by young people of high-school age who seem independent, interested, and hard-working. Youthful instructors work with the students. People move in, around, and between areas with a sense of purpose.

The Des Moines program is designed for students who are

not attending the regular school in the city. Some left school by choice, others left by invitation. They do not attend regular school because their life and learning styles do not match the style of the regular school.

The Drop-In School is an attempt—within the system—to provide an environment which meets the needs of these students. People who need work paced to their speed, teachers who identify with students, lessons which are close to their real life, and adults who accept teen-agers for what they are, are guiding factors.

The program developed over several years. It started as a tutorial program in a neighborhood home. The success of reaching students with obvious school problems encouraged the local business community as well as the school system. But a school counselor wanted a better alternative for ninth- and tenth-grade students who were forced out of school, and found businessmen who would back the venture.

The school system agreed to try an experiment. The school board and other administrators approved an alternative program. The Drop-In School was designed to complement education in the city. It was not proposed as a means of "showing up" the faults of the system. Approximately one hundred students are served by a staff of ten, including secretarial help. The program is financed primarily by the school system, but additional funds are received from private and civic sources.

Businessmen in the neighborhood encourage dropouts to attend. When students first arrive, they may treat the matter quite casually, but they soon see the value of serious work. A student who wants to stay is given all the help ten adults can provide. Anyone who does not intend to participate is politely asked to leave. The philosophy of the school is that if young people are mature enough to walk through the door of the Drop-In School, then they are mature enough to decide to work for the privilege of staying.

THE DRUG ABUSER

There are kids who drop out of school because they decide it isn't doing a job for them, and there are those who are removed for a variety of other reasons. In Long Beach, California, enough children are excluded from regular school for drug abuse that the Long Beach Commission of Economic Opportunities established two storefront schools: one for the excluded drug user, the other for the teen-age dropout. This was done in conjunction with the Long Beach Unified School District so that it is possible for those who attend the centers to receive credit toward graduation. Centers for dropouts are no longer unique, but a center for the drug-abuser dropout is. All students at the drug center are referred there by the Long Beach Unified School District. Referrals to the dropout learning center come from the Neighborhood Youth Corps. Both centers are geared to handle a maximum of thirty students. This number allows the center to maintain a ten-to-one ratio of students to instructional personnel.

The drug center teaches the subjects required for graduation from the Long Beach public schools. The main variance from the public schools' method of instruction is in the facilities. The learning centers consist of one formal classroom and several informal class "areas," which are furnished with a blackboard and couches. Each student has about one-third of his class time in the formal classroom and two-thirds in the informal areas.

Students in the dropout learning center study subjects of practical value to them and also work in local businesses. The center helps find employment for each student. The center pays each student for twelve hours of work per week and for twenty hours of class attendance. Each student, then, puts in a thirty-two-hour paid work week.

Instruction at the dropout center is conducted in small

groups or on an individual basis. The goal of such instruction is to tailor it to the individual needs of the student who is commonly termed "hard-core dropout." It is hoped that a secondary result of the program will be to entice some of these students to return to regular public schools. The reading program of the dropout center is primarily based on Edward Vail's *Formula Phonics* system, but individual programs are established if the student does not respond to this system. The same applies for all other courses.

All of the students at the drug center have been excluded from the regular schools for drug offenses. All students are required to attend a twice-weekly drug program which consists of informative "rap sessions" with an expert in dangerous drugs, such as Lieutenant James Miller, head of the Long Beach Police Narcotics Squad and a trained psychologist. In addition, all students attend private psychological counseling sessions. These sessions are designed to stem the students' use of dangerous drugs. When the counselor feels the student is ready to return to the regular schools, he is returned. About 85 percent of the students have returned. Most remain at the learning center only eight to ten weeks. They are graded in the regular manner for their academic work, and these grades are accepted by the schools. The student thus returns to school without having lost any academic credit.

Both centers incorporate some type of antidrug program in their offerings. These programs are required for all students. The drug center has been highly successful and has never had one of its former students return or be cited by the public schools for an additional drug offense.

Community response has been overwhelming. The Long Beach Public Library, for example, assists the center in many ways. Going to the library is a field trip for the students. They seem to feel it is a free experience and not a part of the school's offerings.

Evaluation at the drug center is by test and written assignment, usually constructed by the individual teacher.

The order created by the no-nonsense policy of the drug learning center seems to give the students some standards of conduct and a sense of security. And those observers who might favor a more flexible class schedule or grading policy cannot argue with the success in rehabilitation that the center shows.

UPWARD BOUND

Upward Bound, a project funded by the federal government, helps high-school students from low-income families develop the skills and motivation necessary for success in college. Students are generally admitted after completion of the tenth or eleventh grade. They live on a college campus during the summer and participate in academic, social, and cultural activities. There is also an academic year component which enables Upward Bound students to have a continuous program throughout the entire year, often including experience in wilderness living.

The on-campus summer program consists of a six- to eight-week session which varies by college and geographical area. It normally emphasizes reading, writing, and other basic communication skills. There are courses in arts and sciences, field trips, and cultural events. Upward Bounders talk with artists and performers, observe various events, and write about their experiences in an attempt to broaden their horizon and gain perspective and understanding. College students tutor them in the basic skill subjects. During the academic year, students are in contact with Upward Bound teachers, counselors, or tutors through meetings, classes, home visits, counseling sessions, or tutorials.

STREET ACADEMIES

The Urban League has set up more than seventy centers that try to work with educationally alienated youth, ages sixteen to twenty-one, to prevent them from becoming total dropouts at age twenty-five.

The Urban League educational activities are designed to help build a base for equal opportunity through education. Tutorial programs, Street Academies, and counseling programs are only a part of the effort to mobilize community support. Drawing the dropout back into society has long been a focus of the League. For example, in New York City in Harlem, Bedford-Stuyvesant, South Bronx, and the Lower East Side of Manhattan, Street Academies are serving to achieve this goal. These non-accredited academies offer those who do not wish to return to the traditional school setting an opportunity to continue with some education. Instruction is provided for all grade levels, and students are met on their learning level.

Cleveland has a program on three levels in which students progress through programs that may lead to a degree granted through Case-Western Reserve University. Circle Prep is the name which identifies the Cleveland program of basic education, continuation and completion of high school requirements, and—if the student desires—college preparation. The program serves to counsel students into appropriate education programs which meet their goals.

The educational program of an Urban League Street Academy is designed to be relevant to the students' lives. It is also intended that the academies be a help to public schools through the demonstration of good human relations and educational practices.

The National Urban League, recognizing its responsibility

to those who have been pushed out of school, aware that only through the offices of a national body can a program like Street Academies have a far-reaching effect, adopted the Street Academy projects and now provides necessary know-how to its affiliates by helping them get a program started.

Concluding that the average ghetto school is a failure factory, the New York Urban League created its own system of education through the Street Academy program.

The program is divided into three stages—Street Academy, Academy of Transition, and Prep School.

Street Academy. A Street Academy is usually a storefront school, conveniently located and dedicated to motivating and stimulating the dropout to revive his interest and need for an education. Individualized study programs permit the student to stay until he reaches the eighth-grade reading level. This prepares him for Stage 2.

Academy of Transition. In the Academy of Transition, the student begins to work with the traditional courses, with emphasis placed on basic subjects that were covered in Stage 1. Depending on his ability to handle these subjects, the student prepares for entry to Stage 3.

Prep School. The Prep School is a springboard to college entry. Students are assisted in developing new and more effective work and study habits. Self-discipline and enhancement of skills and talents are stressed through special techniques that include group inquiry. Self-determination and pride in achievement are the keys to success of this program.

Recruiters roam the streets night and day, approaching potential candidates for these schools. They haunt pool rooms, street corners, drug addicts' hangouts (called "shooting galleries"), cajoling, pleading, persuading youngsters to give education a try. They are a dedicated and fearless army of young men whose greatest stock in trade is their sincerity, compassion, and concern. They all share one common denominator.

They understand these kids and talk their language. They truly care, and the kids trust them. Most important, they have the ability to recognize leadership potential that can be developed and hopefully eventually turned inward to the ghetto as well as the community at large.

Once the street worker has succeeded in getting the dropout back into the classroom, the instructor—usually with a B.A. degree—takes over. The instructor himself, however, usually doubles as a recruiter during non-class hours.

Along with the staff recruiters, the students and graduates of this program are its best salesmen. Their enthusiasm is contagious, and many youngsters they meet on the streets are encouraged to apply. Word of mouth also reaches other agencies who refer potential students.

Curriculum. On the Street Academy level the students are barraged with instructional materials, round-table discussions, and selected subjects—including general science, math, English, and social studies, designed to arouse their interest, a necessary first step. The atmosphere is informal—the teacher, black or white, must permit his students self-expression in both dress and hero worship. But the learning activity is intense. The teacher must also be more than a repository of facts. He must develop warm, personal relationships. It's a full-time job. The age range for this level is seventeen to nineteen. In most cases the students are dropouts, but occasionally a student wanders in from the public high school. Another group consists of high-school graduates lacking the academic credits for college entrance. Pressures to make grades are at a minimum, and a youth can stay at this level until he feels secure enough to move up to Stage 2 Transition. Through this level, both resident teacher and other staff are on call at all times.

The Academy of Transition serves as a bridge between the Street Academy and the Prep School. The quality of education is heightened, and it embraces a wider range of subjects.

Sociology, biology, and drama, are introduced. The role of the teacher, however, never varies. He must continue to talk, plead, scold, and mold. The last class bell only begins a new phase—extracurricular activities are encouraged. Pride in achievement becomes noticeable. Sounds of young voices debating—sometimes with faculty—the sounds of an original drama being rehearsed are but a part of the hopeful atmosphere which characterizes the Academy of Transition.

Prep School is the final stage before college. Transcripts are carefully evaluated, SAT scores and cumulative averages are reviewed, and all gaps filled in to give the student the proper credits for college admission on a competitive level. It is usually a two-year course, which includes more intensive and disciplined study of math, from elementary algebra to calculus, African history and culture, and English. Some of the students have progressed rapidly enough to apply and be accepted earlier by a university. But even the few who decide to call it quits after graduation come away equipped with a Prep School diploma, which gives them a fighting chance in the job market.

The students are required to participate actively in some form of community service. Some join forces with the program's street workers, others do assistant teaching or coach athletics—the choice is theirs.

Expected Results. Based on the successful program run by the New York Urban League, expectations are high. As of March, 1968, 34 young men became college entrants, 30 were sophomores. An additional 90 young men and women are now college freshmen, 150 students attend Harlem Prep, and 107 attend Newark Prep. Recently, 25 young men and women got their diplomas from Harlem Prep and 37 from Newark Prep, and are presently attending universities around the country.

The New York City public school system, recognizing

the value of this educational approach, is now cooperating with the Urban League and has instituted Street Academy programs in five high schools, supervised by Urban League staff. This latter fact constitutes one of the Urban League's goals— the creation of an academic atmosphere which will effect a radical change in an antiquated system of teaching.

VISTA VOLUNTEER SCHOOL

Seventeen VISTA volunteers were the nucleus of an effort to make education important to Indians in Rapid City, South Dakota. They engaged in activities intended to motivate children and make education a realistic life goal.

One activity is called S.O.S., which means Student Opportunity School. The school developed from an increasing awareness that tenth-, eleventh-, and twelfth-grade dropouts need help years earlier—in the primary grades if possible, and certainly by junior high. The VISTA volunteers are working with twenty potential dropouts in a program designed to stimulate interest and promote a sense of self-worth.

Volunteer teachers work to affect positively the attitudes of potential dropouts through a program based on student interests. Students in S.O.S. are asked to select courses of study, work on individual programs, evaluate the courses and the teachers, and become involved in their own education. Projects are developed which will challenge the students to take active, creative roles in daily activities and learn basic skills in reading and writing by their concern for political or personal issues. Creative writing led to an idea for a socio-drama staged and presented by students.

One teacher developed a history course designed to make the life of the American Indian more comprehensible. Through this course the S.O.S. faculty hoped to create a sense of self-awareness and cultural pride. Art, music, writing, and geography are included as they relate to the history of the Indian.

The VISTA volunteers in Rapid City also sponsor programs to serve elementary and junior-high students and adults. A surplus Air Force bus transports children from the edge of the city to a downtown center. Parents and local people first served as aides and then acquired the skills to take charge of their own centers.

The adult program of education has several goals. The chief one is to develop a sense of self-worth in adults who have never really succeeded. Reading, basic math skills, and current issues are the base of the program. Success was reflected by positive attitudes of students and their continued attendance.

Work skills are another goal of the adult classes. A class in roofing was conducted in the spring of 1970. A roofing company sponsored the class in basic reading and math needed for the roofing trade. This was an attempt to match school to the labor market.

In each of these activities, the volunteer has devoted his time to bringing more Indian people into the mainstream of the economic and educational life in America. Success has been limited, progress slow, and the frustrations many. Dual culture and bilingualism are real impediments to easy success. And easy success seems a prerequisite for most VISTA programs. VISTA volunteers are usually young people who want to test their dreams of service and social change for a year or two. Thus they engage in an activity of their choice and then may leave it without continuation after they have achieved their own goals. That is not to say the volunteer's service is not appreciated or that his goals are not worthy. It is merely meant as a caution to the inexperienced, idealistic volunteer that many goals involving social change will take years, perhaps generations. Understandable frustration results, therefore, when the volunteer expects noticeable results after one or two years.

The other side of that picture is that the Indians may become discouraged if they see numerous programs start with promise, only to be abandoned after a year or two when the VISTA workers return home. Continuity of objectives and of effort is a necessary ingredient for success. That view ought to be included in the planning and administration of reading programs and other educational programs, especially when they project cultural changes on particular groups, such as blacks or Indians.

ADULT LITERACY

Many young adults (and even their parents) are no longer able to get a formal education and yet have not learned how to read well enough to earn a comfortable living. Some may have dropped out of school and are so heavily burdened with family responsibilities that they could not attend regular school even if they wanted to. Migrant workers, immigrants, those who suffered emotional problems during their regular school years—all face a world where reading may govern the kind of work they can do and certainly will govern the quality of life they lead.

Literacy Action, Inc. While motivation is needed in the younger age group, specific skill development in reading is needed in the older. Adolescents and adults who have not done so often want to learn to read not only to get a job, but to enjoy life more, or to maintain self-respect. Many need individual help at no expense or a minimum expense.

Seeing this need for adult literacy programs, many organizations are providing free tutoring. Literacy Action, Inc., of Atlanta is an example.

Literacy Action, Inc., is an all-volunteer group that works

with adults and children who have not learned to read or who cannot read well enough to carry out ordinary tasks.

It was founded by Mrs. Mary Hammond, who became interested in the problem when her child failed to learn to read. She had set up a school in Roanoke, Virginia, to give her child the kind of instruction that was necessary. When she moved to Atlanta, she organized and directed a group whose goal was tutorial service in reading to anyone who could not afford instruction in regularly established agencies. Once it was established, the organization joined the Laubach Literacy Centers and now uses the Laubach materials as the primary vehicles for teaching. Mrs. Hammond, a former teacher, was trained in the Laubach method and then instructed tutors in Atlanta.

The organization is housed free of charge in the Central Presbyterian Church, 201 Washington Street. Many service organizations use the church facilities for their activities, and the offices and training rooms are attractive and in the midst of a busy church education building. Most of the tutoring, however, takes place at other churches, schools, or other convenient places. The group tries to set up meetings relatively convenient to both the tutor and the pupil.

The tutor receives four half-day training sessions before being assigned. These sessions are seminars in which one of the directors reviews the Laubach materials and trains the tutors by having them perform the exercises. They are shown other materials they may use to go beyond the Laubach materials or to motivate or to meet a specific interest.

There is no one source of money for the Literacy Action group. There is not even one major contributor, unless the Presbyterian Church might be considered for donating space for offices and training. The volunteers themselves buy the materials. The basic kit costs them ten dollars. Funding is a problem, and a board of directors solicits constantly.

Through newspaper stories, radio and television interviews, and announcements in church bulletins, Literacy Action is made known to prospective volunteers and to those who want to learn to read. A student stays with a tutor for a year, at which time a decision is made about his need to continue or to go on his own and keep practicing. Meetings are held twice a week, for approximately sixty minutes.

Because there is no paid help, chores such as keeping the office staffed and conducting the training sessions impose heavy work loads on those who take on leadership roles. Some 1,600 tutors have been trained, and some 500 are active, but funds are needed for full-time supervisory personnel.

Libraries supply materials and books for those who want to become literate, but some people may not realize that libraries can help teach adults to read.

Libraries also assist the nonreader who has minimum skills but refuses to read. Detention homes seem to be filled with this kind of person.

The Philadelphia Free Library offers one example of how a library can deal with that kind of adult nonreader.

A team of young adult librarians provided a program for girls at the Youth Study Center, a detention institution for those awaiting trial. Each week a librarian took a recreational program to the center on topics such as astrology, good grooming, poetry, folk tales, palmistry, Africa, games, and art projects. In addition to the specific program, the librarian circulated paperback books to the girls. The repeated weekly visits by friendly faces, the popular titles, and the interesting programs combined to make this program successful and motivated the girls to read. In the beginning, the girls had been labeled as reluctant readers. As the visits progressed, they reached avidly for the books, related the plots enthusiastically to the librarians, and traded the books among themselves. They also became more relaxed in reading aloud during the programs.

Further, the influence of this library program caused them to publish their first newspaper.

A team of male librarians provided a similar weekly program to men awaiting trial at the Philadelphia Detention Center. The librarians played music, led discussions in black history, and showed films. The topics they presented and the stimulation of their presence motivated the prisoners to take all the reading matter the librarians brought.

The Adult Reader Development Program, funded originally by the federal government as a pilot project, proved so successful that the city of Philadelphia took over its funding as a permanent function of the Free Library. Its purpose is to provide literacy materials to groups who are tutoring adults and young adults in basic education. It provides material in six subject areas of adult interest (the community, family life, jobs, communication skills, science and math, and the world) on first- through eighth-grade reading levels for use by tutors and students. Tutors come to the demonstration collection room, where copies of all available materials are on display, and they select what they need for their programs. They check the materials out for a year and renew them by phone. Further, the students may write in their workbooks. The Opportunities Industrialization Center, the Philadelphia Adult Basic Education Academy, the Philadelphia Tutorial Project, Upward Bound, Philadelphia Detention Center, and the National Teachers Corp., are a few of the many agencies which have used the services of the Reader Development Program.

The Free Library also purchased a mini-van, called the Freewheeler, that operated within the Model Cities area of Philadelphia. It stopped, circulated books, and showed movies on the street wherever people congregated. It was designed to serve adults and young adults and is specifically planned to lead people to use the nearby branches to further their literacy and occupational skills.

Reading Skills Center. Three reading centers were established by the Cleveland Public Library in the main library and two branches in order to develop already existing skills in disadvantaged adults who were functionally illiterate. One branch served a 98-percent black population, the other 98-percent white, both with low educational levels.

An entirely new staff was added, including one reading specialist, a project director, a Spanish-speaking social worker, two part-time recruiters, and several clerks.

The centers were established in available space—a balcony, a basement, a hallway. A movie, *Step a Little Higher,* was made as part of the project evaluation.

Evaluation solicited subjective comments by staff members and also took into account circulation figures. Materials circulated included professional books and easy reading materials especially written for adults. Teaching on a one-to-one basis was found especially effective.

La Retama Public Library. Informal reading programs have also long been part of the Corpus Christi, Texas, Community Action Program. Library workers assist at Community Centers (Neighborhood Centers), basic-adult-education classes, Jobs for Progress, and in the library. Helping prepare people for GED (high-school-equivalency tests, literally, General Education Diploma) is a part of library-staff activity.

The library makes it a policy to encourage the use and understanding of library facilities. One class of adults from Jobs for Progress were given instructions on the use of the library and an introduction to the type of materials available there. Special interest was shown in the records available at the Greenwood branch library of teaching English for Spanish-speaking people. A deposit library was organized in Bishop at the Community Action office. Encyclopedias, reference books, and general fiction and nonfiction were placed in this branch library.

REACHING THE YOUNG

"Under thirty and cool." That label may not describe adequately a group of people, mostly young, who doubt the efficacy and the sincerity of established institutions—of which the library is one. Because these young people want to "look cool" they may not use the regular library services and may miss opportunities to gain a perspective about life that books record.

Some libraries try to attract the young by painting a mod face. The Tulsa Library even has a mod-mobile, decorated with psychedelic swirls. The fact that the library is out on the street with swinging colors and an inviting stance makes a difference to some young people.

The Pittsburgh Public Library also uses a bus and shows outdoor movies using one white side of the bus as a screen.

A library doesn't always need rolling stock to contact the nonuser. Book racks in drugstores or other meeting places, storefront libraries, rap sessions followed by appropriate books are all magnets which attract the nonreader.

A year of activity for Tulsa's mod-mobile was topped off when one of the drivers donned a Santa Claus suit and drove to two of the lowest-income areas. A local distributor of paperbacks and magazines donated books for Santa to give away, and women from a local church served ice cream and cookies. The entire Tulsa Library staff donated new and used toys to the Christmas project. A VISTA volunteer repainted and wrapped hundreds of gifts. On Christmas Eve, a black Santa went to every house in the two neighborhoods and distributed the toys.

During one year's operation, the circulation, including books, records, and magazines from the mod-mobile, totaled over 5,000 per month.

One librarian in Pittsburgh, as coordinator of Project Outreach, brought the Carnegie Library and the people of Pittsburgh's Hill District together. Elizabeth McCombs chose her books very much on their face value. "Awaken interest first, then channel it," was her motto.

The project's main goal was to reach the non-library-user on the Hill, who either had no interest in books or who couldn't get to the library. As much red tape and library formality as possible was cut. A micro-bus transported the books. No library cards were required of bookmobile users. Borrowers simply signed the card in the book.

Workers recruited from the neighborhood came out to help when the mobile unit appeared on their block. With a little training, they were able to round up their neighbors, work in the bus, and tell stories on doorsteps.

Inside the bus, the atmosphere was different from the marble floors and stone pillars of the Pittsburgh Carnegie Library, but many of the same standards applied. All-time favorites such as *Story of My Life*, by Helen Keller, and the Dr. Seuss books were in lighter, more colorful paperbacks. Race and the urban way of life were two prime considerations in stocking books. Picture books for the bookmobile had heroes and heroines from all races and nationalities. Their adventures were in city scenes such as playgrounds and supermarkets. The more mature reader could also find a new hero in his books, including black sports figures, artists, and even a rodeo rider who bucked hardship to find success.

Ceramics and Reading. Ceramics and reading instruction are an unlikely combination of activities, but a group in Springfield, Missouri, used the two to the benefit of reading. By dealing with ceramics and other practical tasks, a project for rural counties in Missouri enabled students to come together to learn work skills and then to learn to read in connection with those skills without feeling self-conscious about their limitations.

The Ozark Area Community Action Corporation (OACAC) program was an adult-education program which served three groups of area residents: young adults, senior citizens, and high-school dropouts. What most of them wanted was a GED certificate, skill training for a better job, or increased and improved social and home life. A seventy-eight-year-old worked for and received his GED diploma. Teenagers took part in a summer reading program that focused first on making ceramic pieces.

OACAC served an eleven-county area marked by rural poverty and traditionally low in educational standards, 94 percent white, 3 percent black, with a mixture of Indian, Mexican-American, and foreign-born making up the other 3 percent. OACAC organized programs that attempted to break down the reluctance of the rural people to go to school to learn to read. One program, however, was a straightforward attempt to achieve the equivalent of a high-school diploma through the GED test.

Evening classes were in churches, schools, and CAC centers. Each of the eleven counties has from one to three classes going at a time, with ten to fifteen students per class. Adult-education subjects were taught, as well as arts and crafts, the latter primarily for senior citizens as a way for them to make some extra money. In the project were twenty paid and twenty-four volunteer instructors, of whom seventeen were state-licensed teachers from the local school systems. All the classes included reading instruction, and the goal of improved reading ability became significantly more important in the community.

Class materials consisted of GED work tests. Students were tested by CAT (California Achievement Test) battery tests of various levels. Quarterly reports submitted to the regional OEO office served to evaluate the progress of individual students and the program as a whole.

In the summer of 1970, OACAC sponsored a program for high-school students. Although the primary subject was remedial reading, arts and crafts instruction was included to maintain the interest and involvement.

One school had 137 students enrolled in a "reading and ceramics" class. A second school, with comparable students in a straight-reading/English curriculum had much less success. Attendance remained high for the students in the innovative class but dropped considerably for the students in the traditional setting.

The reading and ceramics class operates on the principle that students can be motivated to learn through the process of transfer. The student is able to find success in one learning situation. Students begin the day in the ceramics class, then, after working for thirty minutes, transfer to the reading class for formal reading instruction. The students read material which relates to their artwork, and return to the lab after reading class. Reading is sandwiched between active, tactile work that is stimulating and shows tangible evidence of progress.

A program designed to prepare fifteen women for their driver's license tests is an example of how sensitive the program was to the needs of the people. In the rural southwest of Missouri, transportation is crucial for food, school, church, and other basics. Women are often stranded even if a car is available.

The curriculum and text consisted of the state driver's manual. Reading was taught along with the laws, rules, and principles of good driving. The women received practical instruction in driving and learned to read at the same time. Success in reading can be estimated by the success of the class: all fifteen women accomplished the goal.

MIXED AGE GROUPS

Many programs gather a variety of ages together for instruction. They sometimes try to work with entire families, such as the migrant worker program in the southeastern part of Missouri. In Springfield, Missouri, a project pulls in both high-schoolers and adults for reading instruction in eleven counties from southwestern Missouri.

Programs don't always evolve into the same pattern that they had in the beginning. A literacy program in Atlanta, for instance, started as an adult literacy program and soon became a mixed group when more and more children were referred to the tutors. When asked about that shift, some tutors said they were trained to tutor in reading and after that it was people that they were to serve, regardless of age. No one can fault that attitude, but it is doubtful that many volunteers have a broad enough knowledge of materials and learning techniques to shift over large age spans. What seems to happen with most multi-age programs is that some volunteers specialize in one area, some in another.

In the descriptions that follow, note the manner in which these programs teach reading for different age groups.

Orange Community Action Association—Orange, Texas. The Orange Community Action Association is a volunteer agency funded by the local United Fund. The greatest share of one budget goes to pay the salaries of two part-time receptionists, one of whom also works two nights a week as co-ordinator of the Learning Laboratory. The budget for elementary tutoring and summer program for children is $200 per year. The same amount is allowed for repair and replacement of equipment for the adult learning program.

The adult-education program has a Learning Laboratory in a community center which uses self-instructional materials exclusively. Besides reading, instruction is offered in many of the general subjects taught in secondary schools. The purpose is to prepare adults for improved employment or self-enrichment. Most of them want to pass the GED test or other tests for employment or vocational training. Most of the adult students have poor reading skills and thus concentrate on reading improvement first.

Some of the materials are: *Programmed Reading for Adults* (McGraw-Hill); *Sullivan Reading* with tapes (Behavioral Research Laboratories); *Reading for Understanding* kit (Science Research Associates); and *Controlled Reader Jr.* with accompanying filmstrips (Educational Developmental Laboratories, a division of McGraw-Hill). *Lessons for Self-Instruction in Basic Skills* (all levels) prepared by California Test Bureau has been quite successful with adults and some of the children. They like "those little books that talk to you." *Imperial Aural Junior High Reading Program* (tapes and books) prepared by Imperial Productions has also been popular.

A tutoring program for schoolchildren has two phases. During the winter, children are helped with their regular schoolwork. During the summer, adult volunteers and Neighborhood Youth Corps girls help tutor the children in reading. For the first-, second-, and third-graders a Reading for Fun Program aims at keeping the children reading during the summer. They go to the Public Library bookmobile each week with the Youth Corps girls and then read their books at the community service center located at the low-cost housing project.

Children needing special reading help may use the Learning Laboratory equipment under the supervision of an adult volunteer. So many children request practice on the Learning Lab equipment that many have to be turned away because of a lack of space and volunteers.

The Orange Community Center conducted one program

for young children that had three purposes: to improve their logical reasoning, to strengthen their self-image, and to stimulate their imagination. Four adult volunteers conduct the class periods, two in each class of eight. The class devoted to reasoning was called the Thinking Class; the one devoted to imagination, the Story-Making Class. Each period lasted twenty minutes, and both groups take both classes, followed by ten minutes of verbal reasoning games. The stories and poems from the children are distributed for all the others to read and illustrate with original drawings. The children seem to be enchanted.

No formal evaluation measures are used systematically.

MAMOS (*Missouri Associated Migrant Opportunity Services, Inc.*). MAMOS, a program funded by the OEO, helped migrant and seasonal farm workers from several rural counties in southeast Missouri to make the transition from the field to the factory. It does this through a twenty-three-week program of skill training, education, family services, and employment counseling.

More than 270 men were employed in one year, and four went on to college as a result of MAMOS training. They represented about half of the total enrollment. According to MAMOS statistics, the average trainee entered at second-grade functional level and graduated at "sixth grade plus." The beginning of employment does not mean the end of education, though, for MAMOS encourages former trainees to continue participating in evening classes.

This is typical of the MAMOS philosophy, which is people-oriented. Although the program centers around the trainee, the family is treated as a unit. While the migrant receives preemployment training and upgrades his education, he learns money management and community responsibility. His wife has available classes in adult education and modern home-making. Each family member gets individual attention and services from the MAMOS aides. Thus the family unit is reinforced so that when the man becomes employed, the whole family can successfully cope with the numerous changes in its living pattern.

Five administrators and six clerical people staff MAMOS, along with fourteen paid and three volunteer teachers. Currently there are six MAMOS centers in four counties.

Trainees are recruited through the Supportive Services department, which also provides follow-up service and dental and medical care for the trainee and his family. To qualify, the prospective trainee must have been employed only on a seasonal basis and derive 50 percent or more of his income from agriculture. The total income must be below the poverty level established by the federal government. He must be unemployed at the time of application. Priority is given to men with the least wage income, the largest number of dependents, and the lowest educational attainment. About 52 percent of those accepted are white, and 48 percent are black.

Once accepted, the trainee receives a weekly stipend while he learns a skill and attends classes. MAMOS believes in learning by doing, so trainees get plenty of practical experience, and a trainee who is ready for an available job before the twenty-three-week course is over immediately becomes a taxpayer instead of a tax receiver.

The newly employed man is still eligible for nonpaying evening classes, which, like the regular trainees' and wives' classes, are held in the abandoned school buildings in each project town. Skill classes are given through MDTA (Manpower Development and Training Act) in Sikeston and Tri-County Trade School in Malden.

All but two or three instructors are local people who have high-school diplomas. A few have some college credits, but none is a state-licensed teacher. This is a deliberate choice on MAMOS' part. "We found out that in training adults, we can't

always be concerned with theory. The teacher must be someone who can relate to the trainee's everyday situation," an official explained.

Reading is taught as an integral part of the various adult-
education courses. Various techniques are used. Some centers
have filmstrip programs and mechanical equipment. Others
offer individual instruction, or teacher-made materials. The
teacher-to-student ratio averages one-to-fifteen.

A report is submitted monthly to the MAMOS state office
in Jefferson City. It includes formal and informal evaluation
of students' progress. The trainee is formally tested within the
first two weeks after his acceptance, and every two months
thereafter. Teachers also use an evaluation form to check attitudes and behavior changes.

Success is estimated in several ways: the number employed,
increased self-confidence in the man, more positive attitude toward learning. Others check to see if he has been given
the tools of self-survival in his society. A program official
wrote:

> We don't use "Look, Mother, look. See Mary go,
> etc." For example, we take a foreman's application
> blank with all the information on it; we teach the trainee
> the words and what they mean—how to figure it out.
> Our reading program teaches the trainee to read the
> materials he's going to be faced with today, and daily.
> In driver's education, which is very important now, a
> lot of people have cars but they don't have driver's
> licenses or insurance. They know the skills and can
> drive, but they don't have the education part. So we go
> into the theory of the driver's tests. In certain situations
> they sometimes give oral tests. That's good, but you must
> know how to read afterward—road signs, etc. Nobody's
> going to be there to help. This is very important in our

reading program; we go into that area. We include anything that's going to be relevant to that man's life.

The MAMOS program has been organized to coordinate many services of the county and the state. The education component is designed to complement other activities. For example, in an attempt to make education meaningful, an effort is made to determine specific needs in the community. According to its director:

> We have an industrial relations man who makes contact with employers. His whole job is to go to industry, get information, and then feed it back into the classrooms. He actually brings it back to the teachers and principals so they know what is available, what skills are needed. Then we had a job coach who talked with the trainees and got them ready. He knew what was required, what kind of persons were needed. He talked to groups and individuals; he knew what he was talking about. The information got down to the trainees. The supportive-service workers also knew what was going on and tried to get the family ready— for instance, if they needed to relocate, etc., what the wife should be thinking about.

The MAMOS program is an attempt to bring education to the rural "Bootheel" of Missouri. It is truly a program that takes classes to people—on farms, in small communities, and in libraries, churches, or wherever. Basic skills are taught first —reading, job attitude, basic math, and citizenship. Job placement is a major means of evaluation. Second to that is evidence of growth in the student's self-image or sense of the future. The clarity of direction and the fact that objectives are being measured energetically speaks for itself.

JOB CORPS

All Federal Job Corps centers have had a uniform reading program which was developed by Job Corps headquarters personnel in Washington.*

Conservation Centers are located in rural areas on federal lands. These centers work with male Job Corpsmen who possess minimal reading skills. Enrollees with reading skills above the fifth-grade levels are assigned to Urban Centers, where the programs place heavier stress on vocational training. Conservation Centers emphasize literacy training and the development of appropriate social skills and work habits.

At each Conservation Center there are some Corpsmen who read reasonably well—up to about a fifth- or sixth-grade level. There are Corpsmen who cannot read at all, who do not even know the names of all the letters of the alphabet. There are Corpsmen who learn readily, and those who do not. There are Corpsmen who are eager to learn, and Corpsmen who are not. Any reading program which hopes for at least a minimal chance of success must take into account all of these conditions.

Late in 1964 a Task Force headed by Dr. Douglas Porter of Harvard University designed a program to function under the rigorous conditions imposed by the Job Corps environment.

According to Porter, the program did not reflect any particular theory. It was assumed there were many ways to teach

* This summary is based on excerpts from a speech given at the International Reading Association Convention in 1968. While the concept and organization of the Job Corps centers has been changed in the intervening time, it is clear that the reading program described here has had a great impact on both school and out-of-school reading programs. Principles stated in this description are applicable today to both organizers and participants in outreach programs.

reading, and the program concentrated on using the best instructional materials available.

The materials were such that trainees at all reading levels could be accommodated. In order for the program to succeed, it was necessary to place the responsibility for learning on the trainee as well as on the teacher. While this is hardly a revolutionary idea, it is something that is rarely practiced. However, the Job Corps reading program absolutely cannot function well unless the teacher is willing to share this responsibility with those being taught.

Another important aspect of the program was that it was designed for individual rather than group instruction. Here is another indication that the traditional role of the teacher must change if this program is to succeed.

Program Elements. The program consisted of the following elements: (1) A series of placement tests designed to determine the optimum starting place of the trainee. (2) A set of self-instructional, programmed materials, designed for Corpsmen deficient in basic reading skills (roughly, below the third-grade level as measured by standardized reading tests). Success in these exercises led directly into the graded reading selections. (3) A set of graded reading selections materials (about 2,000), carefully identified by reading level and story content, designed to meet the interest and abilities of a wide range of Corpsmen. (4) Comprehension tests designed to allow both trainee and instructor to determine progress at short, regular intervals.

While experience has introduced new elements, the program still operates essentially in the following way: When a trainee arrives at the center, he is given a short reading placement test. On the basis of the test, he is placed at a specific level in the reading program. The Corpsman then progresses through the program as rapidly as his interest and ability permit.

The heart of the program originally consisted of over 2,000 graded reading selections that ranged in difficulty from about third through seventh grade. Corpsmen who read below the third-grade level use programmed materials until they work successfully in the graded reading materials. Trainees who read reasonably well—above the seventh grade—use materials appropriate to their abilities.

The selections for the graded reading series were chosen after careful screening of all available materials that appeared appropriate in terms of interest for our population. Materials from many sources were utilized. In general, materials were selected that were relatively brief, interesting, and whose content related to the experiences Corpsmen had before coming into Jobs Corps or associated with experiences offered by training and work-experience programs. The items covered a wide variety of topics, consisting of short- and medium-length stories, essays, and nonfiction articles.

The materials were grouped into nine different levels, each level representing roughly half a grade. Grade equivalents are not used in discussing the reading program with the trainees. For example, a trainee is told he is at level three, but not that he is reading at the fourth-grade level.

In addition to being classified according to difficulty, the materials were classified according to interest topics, such as sports, jobs and hobbies, space age, and wild west.

Information concerning the difficulty level, topic, and directions on where the material can be located are found on the master index list. After a Corpsman has been told his reading level, he is free to select any graded reading selection he wishes by consulting the master index list. He simply searches through the titles at his specific reading level until he finds a story he thinks he would like to read.

Each selection has a short comprehension check following it. The Corpsman, after taking the test, uses the answer key and marks it himself. In addition, each trainee maintains his own records concerning selections read and scores received in the comprehension check. The instructor personally administers each fifth comprehension check, and checks the Corpsman's performance in oral reading.

New materials were developed and were characterized by mature tone and content; straightforward story lines; and utilization of interest-catching titles, illustrations, and lead paragraphs. The lower materials also tend to glamorize the working world, whereas the upper-level materials are more factual and realistic. These new materials were well received by both Corpsmen and instructors and quickly became widely used in the reading system.

In addition to new materials, experience also pointed out the need for the introduction of new techniques. Instructors complained about the effectiveness of the placement procedures. Accordingly, informal reading assessment techniques became part of the placement procedures. After paper-and-pencil tests indicated the specific placement levels, these placements were confirmed by listening to oral reading of several passages by the trainee at the level to which he was assigned. While there are no data to confirm that placement was made more efficient, instructors were given more confidence in the system.

An interest inventory indicated that Corpsmen like to read about cars, health, and events related to a personal experience. For example, some of the most popular titles were: *Body Building at the Dinner Table, Are You Drown Proof?, The Deadly Cigarette, Is Your Car Safe? Can You Spot the Makes of Cars?, Cross Country Driver, A Job in the Military,* and *They Know If You've Been Drinking.*

Teacher training was a crucial element in the success of the Job Corps program. Instructors were trained before they assumed teaching assignments. They were familiarized with the materials and the needs of the students. Consultants were available after instruction began.

Regional workshops provided current instruction on developing trends in each area being taught. The key to success of this phase of teacher training was using experienced teachers to instruct other teachers. It was found that some reluctant teachers who would reject advice from experts would readily accept advice and suggestions from their peers.

Several other evaluative factors emerged. First, the testing program was not considered to be comprehensive enough. At best, the informal tests gave only clues to the reading ability of the students. Second, the readability formula used for materials probably did not reflect the true needs of the students. Thus, materials were not always initially geared to the appropriate audience. Third, materials were developed and refined over a period of time. Finding the right materials for any population is always difficult. The juvenile format, for example, was challenged as being insulting to the older teen-ager. It was found, however, that the student did not reject it if he thought he would find success with it and knew he would not be ridiculed.

The overall results of the reading program are classified as very good. An extensive body of materials has been developed and is now available for public use. School districts, Community Action Centers, Project New Start in Canada, and the Department of Defense have used the materials in pilot projects. The Air Force has a continuing program (Project 100,000) at Lackland Air Force Base, Texas. Airmen recruits are assigned to the reading program with the intent of bringing their reading level up to the training levels required by the Air Force. In controlled sessions airmen have gained two years' reading growth (from fourth- to sixth-grade level) with 102 hours of training.

The Job Corps reading program has several implications. First, dropouts and other underachieving readers can learn with this system. Second, the programmed approach allows people without special training to become successful teachers or learning aides. Third, the materials developed in the Job Corps could be utilized in many other programs.

LOCKED-IN GROUPS

Libraries may not be in the business of rehabilitation, but reading and books often play significant parts in the lives of people who are shut in. Jails, county homes, drug centers, and other institutions that care for troubled and sick people need the kind of service libraries can give. The Alameda County, California, library participated in a service project that might be labeled "bibliotherapy."

Volunteer readers from the library participated in a reading activity at the County Prison, Juvenile Hall, and County Hospital. A panel discussion on the use of bibliotherapy in a mental hospital planted the seed. From that point on, the program evolved as an attempt to open lines of communication between people. In summary, the program had these elements:

1. Purpose: Therapy through seeing other's problems in books and relating it to oneself without pressure. Open discussion where nothing is expected or required.

2. Training: The volunteers made two visits to Agnews, a state mental institution, participating actively in groups headed by different leaders. They discussed bibliotherapy with the librarian who initiated it at Agnews, and they read many short stories to select those for future use in sessions at the detention home.

3. Location: Volunteers then met with inmates once every week in small groups. A short story was read by the leader. After reading, the leader does little talking, only occasionally asking a leading question to stimulate ideas. Silence must be

ignored. Give-and-take between participants can go as far afield as wanted. The short story is only a springboard. The same group should meet regularly to promote intimate relationships.

The service of the Alameda County Library bookmobile to convalescent homes represents a personal approach in library work that may be easily overlooked, although it is important in terms of human values. The library called the superintendents of twenty-five area convalescent homes and made appointments if there was any glimmer of interest. The library offered a collection of gift books, jacketed and fairly attractive, to be kept at the convalescent home more or less permanently, and a biweekly visit by a bookmobile, bringing requested books and refreshing the collection with loans from the home branch. The library expected, in turn, the services of the activities director or other staff to help locate persons who could use the service and inform the library of new patients, storage space conspicuous enough so patients could have easy access to the general collection, and some kind of cart to wheel the offerings from room to room. Ten homes expressed an interest.

The permanent collections did not work. Having read the books, the patients saw no point in keeping them around, said they got tired of seeing "the same old books," and frequently talked the convalescent-home staff into taking them away. There also was not enough room to continue adding to the number of permanent books. The library received little cooperation from the busy staff members, including the administration, and the library staff and volunteers took it upon themselves to go from room to room finding interested people. And, needless to say, carts were never procured. The volunteers carried books.

Simple as it may sound, the service to the convalescent homes required an enormous amount of behind-the-scenes work. Each bookmobile leader had five institutions that were her responsibility, from the selection and collection of books to keeping card files and reference material. During the two weeks between runs, the leader searched for books of interest to her patients, often scavenged from all over the system; filled out inter-library loans on special books her patients requested; occasionally wrote letters to the administrators or made appointments with them; sorted the returning books and maintained the clerical end of the convalescent service; and lugged innumerable cartons of books around.

The volunteer leader kept a card on each patient, his reading preferences, books he received, etc. The records helped identify the interests and the "moods" or reading atmosphere of a place.

The following account by a library volunteer gives a sense of what work in the convalescent home means:

When I first started seeing Mr. Butts, he was interested in light nonfiction. I brought him Gerald Durrell's animal stories, Sally Stanford's *The Lady of the House*, early California. He began to work on a family history, since his grandfather had been one of the founders of a mining town in northern California. I brought him books on California mining towns, California history, settlers of California. Then he wanted information on the Woodrow Wilson Non-Partisan League, of which he had been one of the original founders. Then he asked me for an obscure book on the life of a certain Indian, which a friend of his had written. He was delighted that I was able to get everything he asked for. Then he began watching a television correspondence course on comparative religions every morning. He asked me to get him some books on Eastern religion every morning, which I did. Noticing how eagerly he delved into them, I asked if

he was acquainted with the *I Ching,* a sacred book
from ancient China, for which I, personally, feel a
great deal of reverence. He didn't know of it, but was
interested. I got it for him, along with an excellent
essay on it by the translator's son. Our personal realms,
philosophies, were beginning to meet. The writings of
Carl Jung have been very influential in my own life,
and I brought him Jung's *Memories, Dreams,
Reflections,* which opened up a whole new area of
thought to him. He was impressed with Jung's faith,
with his belief in the integrity of man's subconscious.
He read *Man and His Symbols* and had long talks
about this man who was becoming so important to
both of us. And as I leave, he shakes my hand and says,
"How can I thank you? You have been my eyes, my
mind, my teacher."

Reading for Addicts. The Lee-Whedon Memorial Library
of Medina, New York, a central school district public library,
serves a population of 12,000 as well as the residents of the
nearby Iroquois Rehabilitation Center of the New York State
Narcotics Control Commission. Residents of the center are
brought to the library under guard each week. The Swan
Library of Albion, New York, serves the Albion State Institution and Correction facility in a similar manner. The Albion
institution houses females sixteen to thirty years old, one-
quarter of whom are addicts. In both cases, the institutional
libraries are inadequate for the needs and interests of the residents.

An innovative program was originated when the director
of the Lee-Whedon Library received a cadet internship grant
from "Library Careers." The Board of Trustees from the two
towns decided to reconstitute the libraries. The cadet intern,
with the aid of both library staffs, purged old books, pur-

chased new paperbacks, arranged interloan service for both inmates and staff, promoted the use of audiovisual materials, and trained inmates in library skills.

By combining resources and staff, the libraries were able to serve their communities and the inmates of the state institutions. Once the inmates knew what was available, they made extensive use of the loan system and used the library as part of their internal education program.

5 ⅗ Operating Principles and Patterns

Fᴿᴏᴍ ᴛʜᴇ programs described in the preceding chapter, several fundamental principles and patterns of operation emerge.

PRINCIPLES

Consider first the general approach toward working with very young children, then with students in the elementary-school age group, and finally with the thirteen-plus and adult population.

Early Childhood. Parents, teachers, and others helping preschool children should be flexible in their attitudes toward children's readiness to read as toward their earlier efforts to walk and talk and use the toilet. A setting—the child's total physical and emotional environment—that provides warmth, caring, continuity, and security is a better culture for growth than one in which the child is shoved into learning how to do something to satisfy some adult's ego.

The National Institute for Mental Health has tested appropriate and effective ways in which parents and volunteers can help children ranging in age from fifteen months to three years.

Their research can be summarized as follows: studies of intellectual development have found no difference in mean mental test scores of infants from different social classes and different races up to fifteen to eighteen months, but by age three large differences emerge. Several studies show that intellectual level is highly correlated with verbal abilities and that the culturally deprived and bilingual groups score lower on verbal tests. Studies of children from the lower socioeconomic levels show they receive less verbal stimulation than middle-class children and that their parents present less adequate models for language learning. These studies suggest that culturally deprived children develop progressively greater deficits in intellectual functioning from fifteen months to three years—the period of early verbal development—because of lack of adequate intellectual, particularly verbal, stimulation.

Tutors and volunteers in a project called Infant Education Research Project tried many activities with young children, and here are a few they felt were most successful.

1. Several objects with which the child is familiar are placed in paper bags. These include toy cars and animals, pencils, buttons, brushes, etc. A game is played, in which the child must reach into the bag, handle the objects, and name them sight unseen. The child can remove and play with objects he can name. The tutor guides him or provides hints for naming the remaining objects.

2. Children need to see that books are part of their lives. Books had already been presented to the children as early as sixteen months of age. At two their attention span still seemed too short.

To increase the span, the tutor selected books that appealed to children. The most popular were books that had big, colorful pictures the children could recognize easily—familiar animals (cats, dogs, birds) and foods (apples, oranges). The tutor presented these books at each session. Sometimes the child received pleasure simply from turning the pages. The tutor named pictures and imitated animal sounds if the picture were an animal. The boys especially enjoyed the animals. Sometimes the child liked to pretend he was eating the food shown.

The child and the tutor took books on walks to show the pictures represented reality. On seeing a live dog, for example, the tutor showed the child a picture of a dog. A variation was to chase or feed animals pictured in the books (i.e., squirrels and elephants). Books with pictures about a family provided similar stimulation. Each picture was named after one of the child's family members. A family game set helped to make the learning more fun. Each figure in the set represented a member of the family (boy, girl, mother, father). The children had fun naming each figure or, sometimes, just knocking them over. Sometimes a child would take a figure to his parents and say its name. If he could not name the figure, the mother would tell him.

Books were made and left in the homes. The child and tutor cut out pictures from magazines and made their own book. Other books the child enjoyed were also left in the home. Sometimes the older children became interested in the books and helped the younger one name pictures. This was another effective method, because the preschooler usually imitated his older brothers and sisters. The child was praised whenever he could name, imitate, or recognize pictures. This encouraged him to make an effort to learn and to speak.

3. Tutors found that lively interest moved from picture books (at age fifteen months, when the project began) to story books (beginning at about twenty-eight months). Some felt much more successful with realistic books than those which de-

picted animals in human dress engaging in human activities, presented inanimate objects (e.g., airplanes) as being animate, or presented nursery rhymes which contained many words for which referents were lacking, (e.g., curds and whey).

4. Another tutor noted that at the beginning of the project, toys were the major instructional vehicle. As the children matured, however, books became more important. At first, even picture books were ignored, and became of interest only after sufficient handling and naming content. A picture of a ball, for example, was ignored until the child had played with and named a real ball. The tutor reported the most effective books at this early stage were those dealing with sensations, or those having large and brightly colored illustrations. As the children grew, they became increasingly interested in cars and buses they saw while walking with the tutor. Durable, cloth-bound books were left in the home as reminders of what the tutor and child had done together.

These four are only a few practices the Infant Education Research Project felt met the experience needs and provided the language practice needed to overcome the environmental problems often found among the poverty-stricken and the uneducated.

What emerged from the activities of the volunteer tutors in the Infant Education Research Project was not unique. The value of the project was identifying and confirming what works at various ages. There is no magic formula, but knowing what is successful for someone else gives a volunteer something promising to start with. By using similar techniques and materials, one has a better chance of succeeding. (Further details on the Infant Education Research Project can be obtained from the National Institute for Mental Health, 5454 Wisconsin Avenue, Chevy Chase, Maryland 20015.)

The preschool years are times of unrivaled mental and physical growth. Especially in language and concept development it is a crucial time for those contributing toward a child's success in reading. A child's vocabulary, facility with language, variety of experiences, and overall comfort in using language form the base from which reading skills and habits will blossom.

Often closely associated with the language base is the attitude the child has toward himself as a learner, even though he has no formal concept of what a learner is. Thus, preschool reading programs in which volunteers participate may attempt to prepare a child directly for reading in the primary grades, or may try to prevent failure in reading by working with the children early enough to reduce the chance of language and communication deficits by age five.

Volunteers will find openings in cooperative nursery schools, Head Start centers, church day-care centers, community centers, school programs, and private centers. Opportunities include working with special groups—sometimes divided by income, by language, or by race.

Learning in the Elementary School. Teaching reading, writing, and arithmetic has been the function of the early grades in the elementary school since its inception. Teachers, parents, and children expect reading to be learned during the first two years. If it isn't, the consequences for the child are often crippling, and the longer a child fails, the less chance he has of ever succeeding. He has too much working against him —a feeling of failure, the social stigma, the inability to carry on in other subjects for lack of reading skills, and the growing gap between what he can do compared with his classmates' achievements. Some observers feel that by the fifth grade irreparable damage may be done to a child's school career if he has met continued failure in the early grades.

Walk into most primary-grade classrooms and you will find the children working in small groups, reading aloud to the teacher, working in their reading workbooks, or reading silently to themselves in order to answer questions about the passage assigned to them. Typically, the books lead them sequentially through a variety of skills and through an ever larger vocabulary. Each child moves at a pace that fits most of the group or that fits the temper and judgments of the teacher. The individual child does not get much time to read aloud so that his responses are heard by the teacher. The teacher must look after the needs of all the children and might not notice an individual making incorrect responses.

It becomes clear, therefore, that a child can move month after month in school, year after year, without mastering the vocabulary, the word-identification skills, or the comprehension skills he needs to become a competent reader. Like everyone else, he gets caught in the system, moves through it as a semifailure, and cannot escape. He doesn't have the authority or the will to shout for help—at least, not in an adult sense. But he often seeks help in his own way. He misbehaves, feigns illness, plays hooky, or day dreams during the work periods. By the time he reaches fourth grade, he is convinced he cannot do well in school, and his teachers probably agree. "Maybe he should be put in a slower group," they say. But what is the slower group doing in the fourth grade? They are using the fourth-grade reader, simply going through it at a slower pace. What the failing child needs is to understand concepts and to get the kind of reading practice he failed to get as a first-grader. The slower fourth-grade group doesn't hit the mark at all.

All of this happens without malice. No one has a grudge against the child. He fell victim to the system—a system filled with good people, sincere teachers, friends, and school buildings filled with attractive facilities and books. But it is a system that isn't geared to looking at children as individuals and has not used the basic principle that children need success regularly to continue to want to learn.

The happy turn now occurring is that both schools and outside agencies are designing special programs, often using aides and volunteers to complement the school work and help children get the encouragement and the practice that they need to achieve success in reading.

Success for the Child. What does it mean for the child to succeed? Think about learning in human terms. If he were your child, how would you react to his attempts to learn? When he learns to catch a ball, for example, each time he succeeds, you clap your hands and say, "Great! Do it again." And if he fails, you say, "Okay, try it again. You almost made it!" You don't tell him to go sit in the corner with the rest of the dumbheads. And if he repeatedly fails to catch the ball, you say to yourself, "Maybe we should start with something simpler so we can get him ready to catch the ball. He'll catch the ball later."

An adult took time with a child to practice. He encouraged him in his successes and glossed over his failures. In effect, the child was seeing that he was important enough to merit time and that the adult was not going to hurt him. "I believe in you," the adult was saying to the child. "I guess I ought to believe in myself," the child was saying to himself. The need for that kind of encouragement in learning varies from one child to the other, but it is in all of us.

What, then, in the first or second grade? It is this: "I am one child in a group told to do some things. Sometimes I don't understand the directions or don't understand what we are attempting to do. I can't remember that whole list of words in the space of time the teacher gave us. I admit it the first couple of times when she asks who has their work done—'I don't'— but when I see that the effects are not pleasant, I soon stop admitting it. I hide in the crowd. No one will notice." And he is right—at least for the moment.

Now, think of what happens when your child is hurt. If he shows up one afternoon with a scraped leg or an upset stomach, you comfort him, wash the wound, and apply medicine that will help heal. His body is not in its normal condition, and so you adjust to help. Mostly, though, you try your best through watchfulness and care to keep him in good health so he doesn't have to suffer sickness and pain. In school, shouldn't it be the same? We want to establish programs that enable the child to learn to read, and we want to keep close watch on him so that we can tell when he is in trouble. When some small trouble arises, we counteract it with quick and simple remedies to prevent it from growing into an educational illness that is difficult to cure. That's the way you want your child to be cared for in school.

Volunteers for Success. Many classroom aides and volunteers are providing feelings of success and importance for the child. The volunteer is able to provide response to a child who needs encouragement and who needs to be reminded he is worth something. Someone is willing to donate his time to him alone and say, "I believe you can do it." Most volunteers contribute more to a child's well-being, but that response alone is extremely valuable.

Volunteers also give the primary-grade child the opportunities for additional practice so essential to learning to read. Without regular practice, the child cannot develop automatic responses to written words. Without being able to respond automatically to hundreds of words, reading is difficult and frustrating. If every child could spend thirty minutes twice a week reading to a volunteer who helped him with words he didn't know and who reported his progress to the teacher, a tremendous preventive system would be operating. The individual practice would prod the child to learn while he has the time and the help, and the symptoms of trouble would be identified as soon as they appeared—not months or years later. An alert teacher could act immediately to correct any problems.

The primary grades also are the time when children are most responsive to individual help. This is another reason these grades are the target for many programs designed for elementary children.

The elementary school often has a community sense about

it which makes it relatively easy to get volunteers. The PTA frequently can organize parents and interested neighbors as volunteers. In view of what has been said about the importance of responding to the child early and in giving him a chance to practice reading as early and as often as possible, schools and interested groups should consider seriously the use of volunteer "listeners and encouragers," especially for the six-, seven-, and eight-year-olds.

Most programs for elementary-school age groups are related to the formal school curriculum. Volunteers and paid aides usually work with the reading textbooks used in class, using a direct-support approach in helping the child master the required material. But since a psychologically handicapped young reader may have built up an almost impenetrable resistance to "required reading," volunteers may find the key in books responsive to the child's own interests and imagination. The prudent volunteer finds out at the very beginning of the program whether reading for pleasure is to be encouraged, and if so, to what extent.

When the child enters elementary school, his expectations about learning to read are high. If he meets early success, he has a start that will serve him well throughout his life-long learning process. If he fails, he may have great difficulty in recovering. One way of overcoming many of the failures is regular adult contact and encouragement.

Numerous programs stress that technical expertise is not nearly as important for the volunteer as his willingness to give frequent, warm attention to the student. A combination of encouragement and frequent practice with help from the tutor seems to speed the child in learning to read. There are, of course, some problem readers who need specialized diagnosis and treatment, and the volunteer is not expected to fulfill that role. He offers the child what his training and common sense suggest for skill development and a boost to the ego of the child struggling to make headway in the often confused world of learning to read.

Thirteen-Plus Programs. The volunteer who works with people beyond the elementary grades often works in an atmosphere quite different from that of programs for younger children. In one sense it is the difference between working with the "in-group" and working with the "out-group." Most elementary children are in school and feel that school may offer them something of value. In the years thirteen-plus, many are definitely "out." If they haven't learned to read or are having difficulty with learning, they either get out of school or consider school as an exercise in futility.

Most of the programs for the thirteen-plus age group are aimed at those who are out of school, out of society, out of work, out of success. Though some of the out-group may have chosen their situation, many have arrived there because they are poor or black or red or because of some other culture-related reason.

There are youngsters who found it more pressing to earn money than to stay in school. There are those who felt that the school was doing nothing for them, and so they dropped out. There are those who felt that society had no interest in them, and so they drugged out. There are those who immigrated without a reading knowledge of the English language, and so they are out of work or are in low-paying jobs that do not satisfy them. There are those who failed reading consistently during the elementary years and finally gave up in disgust.

To communicate with this group, the school has to change its tactics and some of its content. Society has to find new means for reaching them and helping them become productive citizens. Volunteers, through churches, social action groups, industry, the armed forces, and so on, are alternate agents for locating and guiding them. If school becomes a threat, society has to create a setting where the threat is reduced.

The fact that dropouts in the thirteen-plus group are not in the mainstream of American society is not a reason to consider them incorrigible. To help them, however, the out-group program has to attack the cause of their not learning to read in school. It may mean a curriculum focused on drugs, poverty, and violence. It may mean teaching reading for a specific job market or a vocational-education program. It may mean that learning occurs on an informal basis, that the student comes to "school" less frequently than usual and for short periods of time. Out-group programs often have to lure students into a place and beguile them into learning to read.

To work successfully with this age group it is necessary to understand their sense of pride, which they must protect to live with their peers and with themselves. Maybe their perspective doesn't match ours, but it is one that has been cultivated and shaped and is therefore not easily changed. Our out-group programs might be more productive if we recalled the origins of the problems and what it takes to overcome them. Let's remember how easy it is for a child to develop a sense of failure in school when his language and experience or perhaps his culture and his color are not part of the prevailing standards. White middle-class language, patterns, ideals, and descriptions permeate the books and curriculum of traditional schools. Thus success for certain children may be difficult or impossible. After years of failure, the learner will adapt himself to that condition. He will search for a place where he thinks he can succeed. By working or stealing or copping out, he thinks he will find success—at least it looks better than continued failure in school. A similar, though not as drastic, picture is the case for those who do not intend to pursue a higher education. Even if their school has an alternative to college-preparatory courses, the students are often made to feel it is for the inferior or those who are at the bottom of the heap.

Especially at the teen-age period, the turmoil of puberty and young adulthood is compounded with the frustration and turmoil of their school lives, violence and degradation in society, and apparent injustices. These facts make it imperative for programs to couple skills in reading with personal guidance. The volunteer may have to work longer for a noticeable improvement in skills; he or she may have to work on skills that are directly related to daily living, such as passing the driving-license examination. At first there may not be an enthusiastic response from the learner. But it is important to remember that the volunteer's role often is that of trying to heal wounds that run deep. Recovery takes a long time.

On the other hand, there can also be moments of deep satisfaction. Friendships that recognize the tremendous contribution the volunteer has made will develop. Sincerity holds great value for today's young adult. Literacy skills, vocational training, pride in their own heritage, personal counseling—any one or all may be needed for a program to succeed. The out-group has to be shown how to find rewards in real-life literacy activities.

Working with older adults poses another set of challenges. The key to effective communication, again, lies in creating an empathetic environment in which help is extended in a non-patronizing way. Wherever possible, volunteers should be recruited from the minority or ethnic community they serve.

PATTERNS

Most of the programs and projects surveyed here fall into one of three quite distinct categories—those that support, supplement, or parallel the established, formal educational system.

Supportive programs serve children and young people who are regularly enrolled in school, and take place within the school or school system. They are funded, administered, and staffed by the institution.

Examples of these are furnished by the programs we have

described in Skamania County, Washington; Seattle, Washington; Cincinnati, Ohio; New Orleans, Louisiana; Saginaw, Michigan; Racine, Wisconsin; Birmingham, Alabama; and Fall River, Massachusetts. They are linked by the active involvement of parents or other volunteers, working in close collaboration with teachers and school administrators, *within* the system.

Supplemental programs serve children and young people regularly enrolled in schools, operate in collaboration with the schools but largely outside of them, and are funded, administered, and staffed in a public/private mix.

Examples include the nationwide Head Start programs; the Fresno and Oakland, California, preschools; Home Start in Iowa (which began as a parallel project and was later integrated with the school system); the Perry Preschool in Ypsilanti, Michigan; the special "schools without walls" in Philadelphia and Des Moines; and the Reading is Fun-damental plan.

Parallel programs usually serve those who, for various reasons, are not in school—dropouts and persons who were otherwise not able to complete or continue learning in formal educational settings. These programs are, for the most part, sponsored, funded, directed, and staffed outside of the school system.

The learning component of Sesame Street is one example, as are the numerous public-library programs; Upward Bound; Street Academies and other "alternate" schools; Edison-Little River Economic Opportunity Program in Florida; the Ben Mott School in Chattanooga, Tennessee; the reading program of the Long Beach, California, Drug Center; some VISTA schools; the Job Corps Training Centers; and special educational programs sponsored by business and industry.

Sources of Funding. Public funds—local, state, federal—are the most common source of support in all three categories, although supplemental and parallel programs rely also on the private sector.

A random sampling of the programs already discussed shows these funding sources:

Book Exposure: Local; National Council on the Humanities; Ford Foundation.

Sesame Street: U.S. Office of Education; Carnegie Corporation; Ford Foundation.

Reading is Fun-damental: Local public and private sources; Ford Foundation; Clark Foundation.

Ben Mott School: Local individuals; churches; Community Action Program (Office of Economic Opportunity).

Volunteers in Public Schools (Cincinnati, Ohio): Ohio Disadvantaged Pupils Public Fund.

Breakthrough Bookhouse (Racine, Wisconsin): Johnson Foundation; American Association of University Women; YWCA.

Administration. Out-of-school programs reveal such a variety of sponsorship that no common pattern of administrative responsibility emerges. Experience tends to prove, however, that the group, service club, church, civic or professional organization that *initiates* a volunteer program must be prepared also to accept the administrative, leadership responsibility, in close consultation and liaison with all of the public and private agencies participating in the consortium. This can generally be carried out through a representative steering committee to which a project director reports for policy guidance. Day-by-day operating authority, however, must reside in the director and staff, for obvious reasons. Program or project budgets should definitely provide compensation for some supervisory personnel, and reimbursement for normal out-of-pocket expenses (materials, postage, out-of-town travel) incurred by volunteers.

Program administrators, incidentally, should also be able to advise volunteers on how their services may be used as personal income-tax deductions where proper and applicable.

Evaluation: How to Succeed with Volunteer Programs. What are the ingredients for success in programs where laymen do the work? No magic formula exists. Determining their success is an elusive process, because most are not set up for a systematic evaluation. Even so, it is evident that success correlates with strong leadership, direction, ability to sell the program, and sensitivity to people. There must be a warm sense of interaction among the persons who make up every project.

The response of volunteers to the people they work with ranks high on the list of success factors. So, too, does the ability of leadership to create goodwill and cooperation among volunteers, community people, school people, and other interested parties. Usually this means convincing everyone to concentrate on those who will benefit from the service. Technical training and knowledge are of less value, because no one expects technical excellence.

Success, however, is not a matter of luck. Programs that run smoothly, have competent personnel, satisfied students, and plans for continued operation and change are the programs with these characteristics:

1. Strong leadership and a sense of direction.

2. Regular contact with potential customers and volunteers and the ability to sell the program to them.

3. Training exercises.

4. An attitude that makes volunteers aware of the feelings and concerns of those in the program.

5. An objective that is clear to all participants.

6. Rewards for both students and volunteers.

7. Evaluation and follow-up.

8. Stability.

Not every program has all of these characteristics. Since most have little systematic evaluation built into them, some method of collecting information about daily and weekly decisions is important for improvement. The characteristics listed should not be applied as absolute to every program. Some have greater weight for programs that operate directly with the school reading curriculum, and others have greater weight for programs operating outside the school in a supportive or parallel way.

Types of Organization. The three types of volunteer reading programs are here for purposes of analysis.

The supportive programs are usually maintained by a school system which directs planning, organizing, supervising, record-keeping, and funding. This program is to help the child in a direct way with his daily classes. Supplemental programs offer experiences or services not easily available in the classroom yet beneficial to the work there. Parallel programs provide services similar to the schools', but in different locations or for those not in schools.

These programs are presented only to show their position in relation to the school, which is, of course, the primary communicator of knowledge about reading. Actually, a program may combine several operations. That's fine. The important factor is that a group organize to help learners, and that both learners and helpers know the services that are available.

When success is measured or when the organization wants to make continuing improvements, it is necessary to have some idea of the organization's basic structure. No one can determine his success without a clear idea of his goals. Looking at the difference between the volunteer program and the school program will help clarify goals and help the organization toward their successful achievement. It makes a difference, for example, whether the volunteer's success is determined by the student's achievement on school tests, by the number of books he takes from his neighborhood book cart, or whether he comes willingly to your storefront class when he won't go at all to his regular school.

We have introduced two facets into the notion of success.

One is concerned with organizational characteristics that lead to success, and the other with measuring success.

Let's review characteristics that mark existing successful programs.

Leadership. Examples abound of individuals who took an idea, obtained workers, and sold volunteers and pupils on its value. It takes belief, commitment, and energy to keep volunteers working in a reading program. Selling them on the idea is a major part of the task, but keeping them informed and enthusiastic is equally important. Many programs reported that their continuance depended on whether they could find a leader to carry on. That statement reveals a potential weakness, too. Once a program moves from its initial organization, it should not stand or fall because of a single leader. Hopefully, the program's purpose is strong and clear enough to get several persons interested in seeing it continue and prosper. Thus if one person drops out, there are others willing to take over.

Communication. Both the workers and the students need to know about the program and its services. Successful organizations usually find several ways to publicize their program. Spots on radio and television, announcements in newspapers and church bulletins, and posters in teen hangouts are some that groups have used. Others send postcards to parents or to the school as reminders of coming events or to provide encouragement about the child's progress. Some libraries print a monthly newsnote about their reading activities.

In programs working in the schools as supportive units, students are often assigned because they have been identified as having a need. Although the program doesn't have to sell itself, it should try to give the student a sense of progress and a feeling of success, thus building his desire to participate. In programs outside the school, volunteers have to sell themselves first. Their program must strike a responsive feeling in potential users. Often that requires an actual selling job; for example, the door-to-door storytellers and the book hawkers described in this book.

Just as important as communication with the students is communication among the volunteers. Many of them will not be secure, because they are not reading teachers or librarians. They need a regular flow of ideas and materials to let them know what others are doing and what seems to be working for other volunteers. Some projects send out a newsletter to accomplish this; others conduct short meetings for orientation and idea exchange. Some have experienced members call recent volunteers to discuss their activities. One project losing workers found that the volunteers (who worked with adult illiterates) felt so alone that they quit after a couple of sessions. To solve that problem, the agency developed a telephone system so everyone had an opportunity every two or three weeks to discuss his work with another volunteer.

Training. It is unrealistic to expect a volunteer to help a child learn to read without some orientation or training. He also needs some practice in how to act and what to do when he meets the child. Without adequate training, the layman feels insecure and may not even show up for the first meeting. Training, therefore, ought to have two purposes: to give the volunteer enough practice or knowledge to make the first contacts with a sense of security, and to give him sufficient knowledge so the child may profit.

Focus. Reading is a broad and complex skill. It involves using the child's background, the way he learns, and a variety of skills with words and thinking. A volunteer cannot focus on all of them, and even a trained teacher has difficulty in keeping them in perspective. The volunteer needs a specific focus, a specific area to work on. Successful projects point their staff members to fairly specific things they can do for the children. The Programmed Tutoring Project, for example, directs tutors to use the classroom texts, and the material tells them what to say about every story. No matter what response the child gives, the tutor has a written reply. Some projects aim at teaching adult illiterates through a specific set of phonics materials. The range for the volunteer should be specified.

Reward. In a sense, programs have a built-in system for rewarding the volunteer. As long as the objective is clear and the task manageable, the volunteer knows when he has achieved it. In some instances, it is enough for the volunteer that a child progresses or talks about books he has read on his own. In those cases, the volunteer's reward is intangible, but it is evident to him. In other cases it is good to praise or recognize the people who perform the service. Various means have been devised by successful programs, including certificates for completion of training activities, recognition in a newsletter, newspaper publicity for those who have served several years, recognition dinners or parties, and so on. Probably the best way, however, is to post the results of the volunteers' work—a bulletin-board display or a note that says, "Congratulations! Two of Mrs. Englander's field trips inspired compositions back in school." or "Another one of Mr. Anthony's students passed the GED test. Congratulations!"

Attention should also be given to rewarding the student by letting him take home samples of his work, giving him a book that interests him, sending a note to his parents praising him for his progress, putting him on the program's honor roll, and so on. The reward must be geared to the age of the child. Everyone wants to be praised, but a secondary student might not appreciate his name on the bulletin board with five stars behind it.

Follow-up. Successful programs try to make sure volunteers and students have assistance if they are not doing well. Regular attendance, for example, plays a key role in the student's progress. If either the student or volunteer does not keep appointments, his progress and feeling of success will diminish. Successful programs try to get regular reports on the tutor. They want to know about absenteeism and will check if it occurs more than once. If a tutor drops his assignment, the director must see that the student is not lost by having another tutor pick up where the previous one had stopped. A standard report form that requires little time is beneficial in getting information.

Stability. Usually it takes a minimum income for a program to continue. But that is misleading, because programs do exist where everything is free and no official money is spent to keep them operating. Other programs have varying degrees of support. One program had a foundation supply money to run the office, but pay nothing for materials, which it expected the volunteers to purchase. At any rate, no specific amount of money is needed to run a successful volunteer program. The program can get its stability from an office that has a certain permanency. It may be in a church education center, in a well-kept storefront, in a school, in a library, or wherever. The location doesn't seem to make any difference, and success apparently doesn't depend on where the service takes place. Some programs operate in pleasant, modern facilities while others are literally jammed into dark corners. The size of the program does not make a difference either. Whether ten volunteers or one thousand are involved, success can be achieved.

One characteristic is evident, however. Successful volunteer efforts grow. This feature tends to give the effort more stability, but it brings with it certain hazards. There comes a point when numbers become so large, for example, that a full-time professional is needed to keep the project going. If it has some relationship to a school district, sometimes the district will take over the program and provide funds and management to keep it going. At other times, there is no ready answer. Two women in Atlanta were devoting half their time to an agency that had more than five hundred volunteers. They admitted that their half-time commitment had grown into a full-time job (without pay); something had to be done to keep them from neglecting their families.

About the only thing that keeps some programs stable is controlled growth. They start small and grow only as they are able to train additional volunteers adequately.

Success Formula. There is no success formula. But it is evident that training, communication, and some systematic evaluation are essential in a continuing successful program. The area that has received the least attention is evaluation. Educational evaluation may sound too technical for many laymen to tackle, but it seems crucial to the survival and the success of the entire volunteer effort. And something more than a standardized reading test is necessary to students in these programs, because what has to be evaluated is more than the final product. Volunteerism raises questions about objectives, procedures, program adjustment, and the kind of people best suited to different tasks.

Evaluation of Volunteer Programs. In an attempt to give some direction on evaluating a volunteer program, we have developed the following outline: Evaluation should start with the initial planning activities and continue during the operation of the program. It should not be something done once a year by looking at the children's scores or counting up how many entered and left the program. Those data should be collected, of course, but they represent only part of what is necessary.

There are three major activities necessary to effective evaluation: (1) ask questions that focus on important decisions for the program; (2) use appropriate means to gather data; and (3) establish valid criteria for judging information.

Thus an evaluation system with some major decision questions looks like the following:

I MAJOR QUESTIONS	2 SAMPLE CRITERIA	3 SAMPLE MEANS
1. Are we working on a real need?	Societal goals. Job Market.	Interviews.
2. Are our objectives manageable?	Understandable. Personnel available. Techniques available.	Questionnaire. Volunteer forms. Interview expert.
3. Are volunteers using the procedures?	Check practice with description of procedures.	Observation. Logs.
4. Do the procedures work?	Student opinion. Expert opinion.	Questionnaire observation.
5. Does the product match the objective?	Check with stated objectives.	Tests and narrative records.

The analysis and summary of all those aspects can constitute an evaluation of a volunteer program.

Procedures for Enacting Change. The most effective program will depend on assessment of specific needs and resources. The following points suggest areas that should be considered in establishing a volunteer program:

1. Determine extent of need through survey of children and staff discussions.

2. Establish objectives through staff recommendation and community involvement.

3. Find personnel through recruitment and in-service training.

4. Create facilities through remodeling and new construction.

5. Purchase materials for specific skill development, maintenance of interest, and variety and flexibility.

6. Select children through discrepancy criterion and teacher recommendation.

7. Schedule treatment to child's best advantage which is on a frequent basis.

8. Evaluate regularly child's progress and procedures of selection and treatment.

9. Report results to child and parents, classroom teacher and principal.

(A more comprehensive list of questions about program development is found at the end of this chapter.)

Common Pitfalls. What to do and what to watch out for. The following checklist may help organizers avoid some of the common pitfalls in either the planning or the operation stages.

1. Organization. Failure to define responsibility and authority. In each situation, the question "What is his or her job?" should be answered.

2. Personnel. Training and supervision are essential.

3. Facilities. Failure to provide adequate space. The quarters for the program should be attractively and suitably decorated if possible.

4. Materials. Failure to allow sufficient funds for materials. Often little or no money is allotted for purchase of materials.

5. Selection. Using only standardized group reading tests to select participants. Individual tests or informal inventories should supplement the standardized tests.

6. Time. Too few sessions during the week. Once-a-week sessions of sixty minutes or more are not advisable. Successful programs have proved it is necessary to meet two or more times a week to obtain noticeable improvement over a semester.

7. Terminating instruction arbitrarily. Ending instruction after specific time periods can be a mistake. Instruction should be carried on until the student shows he can profit from regular classroom work.

8. Assessment. Determining progress by standardized group scores. Ordinarily the standardized group test does not measure skills taught in a reading class.

Positive Planning. Complete and successful evasion of the common pitfalls is the result of careful planning. One way to such planning is a series of steps forcing you to think through every facet of the program.

Step 1. Survey the needs related to reading and your volunteer program. What evidence indicates a need for reading tutors? Review test scores; interview parents, teachers, administrators, and students; look for evidence of a need. Telephone surveys, questionnaires, and interviews are best for gathering this information. Find out why people say, "The problem is reading." Find evidence that tutors can help.

Step 2. What resources are available? Make a list of available groups that could support a volunteer program: churches; teachers; students; PTA; Model Cities; federal funds; men's and women's clubs; fraternities; sororities; community action groups; VISTA; professional groups; libraries; others. Include in your list the sources of time, food, money, materials, books, training, talent, political support, and transportation which you can identify. Read the descriptions in this book.

Step 3. Exemplary programs. Find out what others have done. Try not to make mistakes others have suffered from. Contact various groups in your area and in other cities. They can save you weeks of frustration.

Step 4. Alternative programs. Focus your information about needs, resources, and existing programs to establish realistic choices. You may decide that working within the school system is best. You may also decide that a small program conducted on Saturdays in your family room is best. You can make a judgment about the best kind of program after you have gathered as much information as you can.

Step 5. Broaden your base. As you mobilize your effort, plan to use all available community resources. Find out what else is going on. Consult parents and school and civic groups as you develop your program. Do not alienate potentially useful groups or individuals by ignoring them.

Step 6. Set specific goals. Carefully define the purpose of your program. When you set specific goals you eliminate the fuzzy ideas that lead to confusion and inaction. Specific goals should be stated so you know what is to be accomplished. Limits are set, specifying when it is to occur and how it will be measured. For example, "We intend to tutor five children in a ten-week program beginning September 15. Each child will receive two forty-five-minute sessions twice a week. We will supply ten tutors who are trained in reading."

Step 7. Plan program evaluation. There are many methods (tests, opinion surveys, questionnaires, interviews) for gathering evaluation information. Remember, evaluation means gathering information and making judgments about every activity you initiate. A good place to start is by listing your goals, then determining a time schedule which is monitored. Also, itemize the results which would indicate your goals are being met. As you proceed, gather information about specific goals. In this manner you can always know how well your program is developing.

Step 8. Define roles of members. It is imperative that you decide exactly how your program is to be managed. All personnel must have a clear idea of the role of the teacher, the volunteer, the director, the students, and the parents. Educate all members of the project to the behavior they will be expected to demonstrate. Do not let the tutor feel he is replacing the teacher. Avoid creating hard feelings by seeming to make students choose between tutors, teachers, and home.

Step 9. Request school approval. If you intend to organize a program which involves schools, students, or teachers, you must submit a formal proposal which outlines your intentions, usually to the district's board of education. If you have com-

INFORMATION-NEEDS CHECKLIST

INFORMATION

	Needed	On Hand	Not Available
What are the reading needs of local children?			
Do the schools have volunteer reading programs?			
Do I know of good programs worthy of imitation?			
Do I know people who will volunteer?			
How much training do volunteers need?			
What local community groups are likely to sponsor such a program?			
Do teachers encourage volunteer reading programs?			
Do school administrators encourage volunteer reading programs?			
How many students could be served?			
What ages might be involved?			
What kind of program should be tried?			
Where would this tutoring be done?			
What kinds of materials would be needed?			
Where would financial support be found?			

pleted steps 1–8 and have acquired pertinent information, this
should be easy.

Step 10. Begin program. Now that the groundwork has
been established, and the appropriate approvals presumably
obtained, it is possible to begin your program. No two programs are alike, so it is not useful to outline further steps.
However, we must stress the need for evaluation. You must
continually measure progress by the goals you have established.
Evaluation must be a sustained process of monitoring your
program activities.

The checklists which follow provide a useful way to
record needs, anticipate program elements, and begin the evaluation process.

CHECKLIST FOR CONDUCTING A PROGRAM

Has a tutoring location been identified?   _____

Has a training program for tutors been developed?   _____

Has a tutor recruiting effort been outlined?   _____

List the activities of a typical day.   _____

How much tutor time is involved?   _____

How much money is needed for materials?   _____

Are necessary forms available?   _____

Are tutors ready for students?   _____

Do we know why the child wants help?   _____

Do we know what his teacher thinks?   _____

Do we know his parents' attitude?   _____

What will the tutor do the first day?   _____

What is expected of the child?   _____

How does the tutor plan for the second day?   _____

SIGNS OF SUCCESS CHECKLIST

Have we collected information about attitudes from
parents, teachers, students, and tutors?   _____

What special problems have we encountered?   _____

Was the effort worth the product? _____

Did we achieve the stated objectives? _____

Who did not support our effort? _____

Should we try to enlist their support? _____

Has our effort affected the child's school performance? _____

Any signs of good effects on tutors? _____

Do we know the child has improved his reading skills? _____

Has this effort been noticed by the community? _____

6 ❧ How to Succeed with Individual Learners

TIPS FOR TUTORS

No MATTER what kind of program you decide to work in, a key to success is ability to work with an individual. We all have known people who do well in front of a group but who cannot get on with an individual. Most of the programs in this book are concerned with one adult in touch with one learner, as a tutor, a storyteller, a reader, a distributor of books, a listener, a recorder, or many other things. For an example we will discuss some ways a tutor can work with a child to move him toward greater accomplishment in reading. Those who work in other capacities can adapt these remarks.

This chapter of the book will guide you in answering many questions, but it won't answer every situation. Part of the power of having you in education is to take advantage of the imagination and experience you can bring to the learning problem. Ideas here should be adapted to make them fit the individual assigned to you and the setting in which you work.

How am I different from a teacher? The classroom teacher is primarily responsible for planning the approach and the materials for instructing your pupil. He identifies specific skills to be worked on. The teacher is the main planner, while you help the student by answering his questions and making the exercise fit him as an individual. You try to help him gain self-confidence, to see that he can learn to read. You give him the opportunity to practice and indicate that you believe he can learn despite what has happened to him in the past.

You are not an evaluator in the sense the teacher is. In the typical classroom, the teacher judges a child for progress and oftentimes for a grade. A tutor encourages a child to progress but has no intention of putting a grade on his performance. In a sense a tutor and a learner sit down and ask, "How can we work together to overcome some of these problems?" You then proceed without pressure or threat of failure. If the teacher says the pupil does not understand the vocabulary, one of your tasks is to discuss the difficult words and help the child understand. Part of that help may include searching the library for magazines, newspapers, or books that deal with the words and ideas, but in a simpler manner. Thus, in a non-threatening way you provide a real learning opportunity for the child. (This does not say the teacher is a threatening, authoritarian figure, but unfortunately, the child often sees him as a judge.)

What are the differences between the classroom and the tutor room? Making the learning atmosphere different from the classroom may increase your chances for getting the child to read something he couldn't read before, or to feel reading has value for him. In the classroom, there are children who become competitive. The teacher may even encourage a competitive atmosphere. With you, the only competition a child has comes from standards the two of you work out. It's bound to be more relaxed.

When the child performs for the classroom teacher, he has to do so in a limited time in front of other children. A teacher is often concerned with making progress across a number of pages in a book. Consequently, time seems important.

With you a child is not pressured by time, and he performs only for you. You do not have to cover material in a given time. If the child needs explanation or encouragement, you take the time to give it. The classroom teacher is necessarily pressured by the needs and behavior of the other children, but you don't have those pressures. This is not to say you always have control over the atmosphere and the time in which you work. There will be restraints on you, too. But you can permit more freedom than the child is likely to find in the classroom. Hopefully, you will be able to create a helpful atmosphere and pace.

The teacher should discuss the problems of your pupil and guide you in using specific games or materials. You should devise a report for the teacher so he knows what kind of response the child is making. (See Figure 1.) This enables the teacher to follow up in the classroom and to offer additional advice to you. With this arrangement you and the teacher can move forward with more security. If you do not report to a teacher, the form in Figure 1 can be used as a personal log of your work.

Because many teachers have not guided aides in the past, they may not at first feel comfortable having someone else carry out their directives. Take care, therefore, not to threaten the teacher, thereby cutting off essential communication about the child. Some programs have tutors communicate with teachers only through written reports to reduce possible conflicts. Perhaps that seems an overreaction, but it should be kept in mind if problems arise.

How can I prepare for the first meeting with the learner?
No one expects you to have the technical training of a teacher.

Your role is more that of an adult friend with a little more training and background than the person you are working with. Self-assurance is necessary, and it will help you in your first meetings.

Remember, if you have nothing else to offer, you can give the child encouragement. The fact that an adult chooses to spend two hours or so a week with him alone is a valuable contribution to a child's ego and his motivation to learn. Someone is saying, "I believe in you." Probably the tutor's major contribution is that emotional boost. Someone thinks he can learn, and so the child will try his best. That is the attitude you should have and work to develop in the child. In addition, you can contribute solid guidance in learning, assuming you have some knowledge of the skills of reading.

How should I dress? Meeting the child is an ordinary, everyday situation; it is not a time to wear the best you have or try to impress the child with your mink stole. He realizes,

Figure 1

TUTOR REPORT-FORM SAMPLE

Name _____

Time _____   Date _____

Objective _____ (The purpose of this meeting is _____)

Reaction _____ (Here is how the student responded
_____ to idea of lesson . . . .
_____ to materials used . . . .
_____ to procedure . . . . . .)

To what extent was the skill achieved? _____ (What did the child do?) _____

How can next lesson be designed to improve his attitude or his skills? _____

(A form similar to the one above could be placed in a mailbox or on a bulletin board for tutors. All they have to do is to pick it up and prepare to meet the learner. Tutor reports can be returned to the teacher's mailbox—discussions can be held by phone.)

however, that you are an adult and would be surprised if you appeared with your hair in curlers or wearing your golf shoes. Your guide should be that your dress doesn't distract. You may also want to ask the teachers or a director what clothes are suitable.

Get oriented. Visit the school or tutor center before the first meeting with your pupil. Get yourself oriented. You don't want to be going up the down staircase as the bell rings and 1,300 kids come charging toward you. Find out where you will meet and get an idea of what you want to bring for that first meeting.

Many schools are strict about visitors, and you may be challenged. Check with the office before your visit to avoid any rebuff.

It would be helpful to visit the school library or public library to see whether your needs can be met there.

The counselors and the vice-principal might give you some tips about the first meeting.

You might want to know where a restroom is.

What should I prepare for the first meeting? You want the first interview to be relaxed and smooth. Extra preparation makes sense. A general rule is that no single activity should take more than ten to fifteen minutes. You may want to keep the same objective, to accomplish the same skill, but make sure you try to achieve it with a variety of activities. He reads to you; you read to him; he writes some questions; together you discuss ways of answering those questions. Naturally, the age and personality of the child will determine the number of times activities have to be changed.

Have different materials and ideas ready. Outline what you want to try and the time you want to spend. Gather the materials for the meeting and prepare for more than you think you will need—in case your pupil moves faster than anticipated.

Being well prepared, however, does not prevent spontaneous activity if the occasion arises. If the child arrives with something he has read and would like to discuss, fine. One of your primary purposes for being there is to help and encourage. One tutor, for example, was working with a child who wouldn't say more than a mumbled yes or no. The tutor had brought some pictures of prehistoric animals and was asking the child if he knew what they were or that they once lived on earth. The child responded, "No," but the tutor noticed his wonder at the apparent size and ferociousness of the dinosaurs. "Let's go see some of these animals," said the tutor. They went to the local natural-history museum, whereupon the child began to talk about how he would fight dinosaurs if he found any real ones. That incident led to the tutor's recording a story that the boy dictated, and they used it as a beginning for learning words and for becoming interested in the relation of spoken words and printed symbols.

Caution: If you see that several meetings have ended in gab sessions that didn't benefit the reading problem, then it is time to push toward specific goals. The child needs to see that there are goals to be achieved: "Let's learn these twenty words during the next two sessions."

Gather information about the pupil before the first meeting. The teacher, the school office, or the counselor may have information on his home and neighborhood background, his grades, or how well he gets along with his classmates. You may find it helpful to call the parents to advise them you will be working with the child. You are "not a teacher but you have an interest in helping him read." The parents might tell you his interests and hobbies, whether he reads at home, or if he has books there. You can say you want to provide him with some magazines but do not want to duplicate what they have at home. In that manner you may learn whether there are magazines and newspapers in the home. Get permission of the school before calling the parents.

What materials will I use? If you are working in a school

or well-organized program, you will undoubtedly be given
minimum materials to help you get started. As you proceed,
however, you will want to personalize your meetings with the
child and make him feel he is doing different things from everyone else. You can fill that need in many ways: building special
charts, making games for him, asking him to select books from
the library, and so on. But one item that seldom fails is the
newspaper.

Because the newspaper is always available, is inexpensive,
can appeal to a wide variety, and is a real-life activity, we will
use it as an example of how a tutor can apply it to specific
needs of children. Of course, you can use your ingenuity to
apply these recommendations to other materials to personalize
instruction.

*How can I use newspapers and magazines to teach read-
ing?* Headlines from newspapers can be used to teach children
to think about the content of an article. Word-analysis skills
can also be developed from headlines. Headlines are in bold
type and can easily be cut up for word-recognition activities
and various kinds of language games. Have the child try to
put the words together to make sense, or give him the headlines to match with the article it summarizes.

"EUROPE SPLIT ON ELECTION": What does that head mean?
What do you expect to find in the article? Depending on the
background and age of the child, he may be able to infer what
will be in the article. But he may need assistance in seeing how
headlines give the reader a cue to the contents. Point out that
the head enables him to form questions that will guide his reading.

What is Europe, and what is an election, or what election
is referred to? Only with that kind of knowledge can the
learner make sense from the headlines and prepare himself to
read the article. Then he can ask why Europe is "split."

Take the head "U.S. TO LEAVE VIET IN FIVE YEARS." Does

the reader know what "Viet" refers to? Does that head indicate a promise? Is it something that is hopeful, or is it a doleful comment? The headline game is exciting. It calls for the reader to supply information, because the headline usually doesn't make a complete sentence. It sets up questions for reading. It enables you to check the child's comprehension by having him read an article and then select from several heads the one that best fits the article. It also enables you to get some notion of his background for reading and the level on which you can discuss things.

Headlines make reading something related to real life. What the newspaper is talking about relates to everyday happenings, sports heroes, the weather, war, crime, and movies. Reading becomes a vital activity.

"CONGRESS GIRDING FOR LAME DUCK SESSION." A child would have to have considerable experience to get the implication of that headline. It is loaded with images and words that are not common. How could you make it more meaningful? Have the child pantomime a lame duck. The term "girding" goes back to the Middle Ages when warriors girded themselves with armor in preparation for battle. What has all that to do with Congress? Why are lawmakers "crippled"? Certainly, the newspapers and magazines have many items that provide interesting comprehension activities, and they often can give the child material he can handle. The sports page is a good place to start many children. Common sports words can be cut from heads, and the student can underline those words as he finds them in articles. It is like a game that teaches him to recognize words, and shows how those words fit in a larger unit of meaning.

The Comics. Another easy reading activity is the comic page. The pictures enable you to develop the idea of a story, or a punch line, or relate text and illustration. All of these are helpful for reading textbooks. Once again the student sees you are helping him read where it counts in his daily life. Reading is communication. If the tutor keeps that definition in mind, he will avoid some of the pitfalls that using newspapers might hold.

What are minimal reading skills? Reading is done for various purposes. Study is one reason for reading, but many people read for recreation or personal benefits. What does the child need to find basic information and to read for enjoyment? Consider some of the things your pupil might do.

Location Skills. What program is on TV Friday at nine P.M.? The child can learn to use the *TV Guide* in developing chart reading skills. He has to find Friday's schedule, search the column for the hour, and read off the list. Related to that are variations that could make it a question-and-answer game (Which program do you think I should watch at ten-thirty on Friday?), or a search for key words ("game," "Frost"), or a discussion about which channel carries the programs that appeal most to you. All of this could be accomplished in five or six minutes. You can help decipher words that prove too difficult.

If your pupil seems unable to work with the *TV Guide* at first, ask him if he would like to set that as one of his goals. Then say, "In two weeks we will make you a master at reading the *TV Guide*." Run through a couple of quick exercises at each meeting. Encourage him to work on it at home and test him at the end of two weeks to show his progress. That serves as an example of what he can do, and gives you and the teacher an idea of some word-recognition skills he needs.

To read the *TV Guide* he had to learn to respond quickly to the words—to be able to skim over them without hesitation —in order to answer the questions. He learned he had to cue himself to key features of the words and to use sound cues or the shapes of the word so he could answer your questions— especially if you put a time limit on the answers. Make it a game, and he will soon be asking for the *TV Guide* exercise.

You can easily move from the *TV Guide* to other charts or maps. The same principle applies. Locate symbols first on the vertical and horizontal coordinates to locate places. It's a beginning that has no end. And you started with a *TV Guide*.

Table of Contents. By taking a large newspaper such as *The New York Times*, you can demonstrate another important study skill with many reading applications. Ask your pupil to find some hint about gardening in the newspaper. Typically, he will begin searching page by page or at random, not realizing there is a table of contents that he can use. Follow that with other searches using the table of contents. It gives you an opportunity to show him valuable study aids and to work with words and phrases that occur frequently in daily reading.

Using Pictures. No one wants a child to place great stock in figuring out a word by looking at a picture, but pictures can be assets in helping a child comprehend. Pictures give the child a concrete image in determining what the article is about. What if the following title appeared in a book without pictures: "The Opossum—A Special Kind of Animal"? For the child who has not seen an opossum or its picture, the animal could look like anything from a centipede to a jellyfish, with unlimited size variations.

But a look at the title with a picture not only satisfies the child's curiosity about appearance but also supplies a whole new experience to talk about.

Ask the child, "What do you think this story is going to tell us? What's unusual about the animal? Look at his long tail. What other animal that you know does it remind you of? Why is the animal shown with a moon behind it and its young on its back? Use your imagination. What do you think this story might be about, judging from the picture?" In those few statements and questions you have focused the child's attention and asked him to associate the opossum with something already known, perhaps a squirrel.

Magazine ads make great reading exercises. Usually there are illustrations and related copy. You can discuss an ad with a pupil without his realizing you are teaching him about reading. Look at an ad for a battery. Ask the learner, "What does it stand for?" His awareness, for instance, of the General Motors trademark may indicate an alertness about autos or about ads that appear in magazines and on television. You can use the headline to prepare for reading the ad. "What does the head suggest? Now, read the ad, and we'll figure out the difficult words together."

Some children who have specific interests may recognize a trademark, the ideas in the ad, or the whole thing. Others may need additional explanation. With one ad as kickoff, you can ask the learner to bring in ads to be used during the reading lesson. Thus, he brings his own reading material. He can't fail in that.

Have him clip unusual trademarks from newspaper and magazine ads to discuss the use of symbols. Symbols crop up in his reading in all kinds of subjects. An understanding of their use will help him in math, science, and other subjects he reads in school.

How do I know if I have succeeded? Judging success in education is not simple, but here are some guidelines:

1. You know that something is happening if after a lesson the learner is able to do something he wasn't able to do before.

2. The learner ought to give some indication he has a feeling of success. One main goal for tutoring is to create that feeling. Does he give you the impression that he is aware of his progress?

3. Did you encourage him or praise him often for his efforts during the lesson?

4. Did you provide learning in small steps?

If you can answer yes to those questions, the chances are you succeeded in the lesson. There are degrees of success, and you will judge those for yourself as your experience increases. You should conduct self-evaluation after every meeting. Maybe you want to rate each item on a four-point scale and compare yourself from time to time. This is an excellent means for self-improvement.

Evaluate more than yourself, however. The important person in this picture is the learner. You want him to develop a positive attitude toward reading, and you want to help him

EVALUATION OF THE LEARNER

This checksheet will serve as an evaluation of one lesson and a guide to planning the next one.

Child's name _____ Tutor _____
Date _____ Time _____
1. Objective: (The purpose of this meeting was) _____
_____

2. Student reaction: (How did he respond?)
    Rate 1–4 (low to high)
      1. showed dislike
      2. did not respond
      3. responded without emotion
      4. responded enthusiastically
  —— to purpose of lesson
  —— to books and materials (describe) _____
_____

  —— to procedures (describe) _____
_____

3. To what extent was the purpose (skill or attitude) achieved? (What can he do now?) _____
_____

4. How can the next lesson be designed to improve his attitude or skill? _____
_____
_____

WEEKLY EVALUATION OF TUTOR PERFORMANCE
Rate 1–4 (Low to high: 1—low positive feeling;
4—high positive feeling)

Preparation
___ There were specific objectives for the lesson.
___ There was a clear plan on how to carry out the lesson.
___ Materials were there and ready to use.
Meeting
___ A variety of activities kept lesson moving.
___ I praised and encouraged the learner often.
___ I made notes on learner's responses.
___ I showed enthusiasm for our work.
___ I gave the learner an indication of his progress toward his goal.
Follow-up
___ I have a clearer sense of the next steps to take.
___ Total points.

(As a record of progress, you may want to compare totals and individual items from week to week.)

TUTOR REPORT-FORM SAMPLE
(to be returned to the teacher)

Name _____
Time _____   Date _____
Objective _____ (The purpose of this meeting is _____)
Reaction _____ (Here is how the student responded
_____ to idea of lesson . . . .
_____ to materials used . . .
_____ to procedure. . . . .)
To what extent was the skill achieved? _____ (What did the
child do?) _____
How can next lesson be designed to improve his attitude or his
skills? _____

gain the skills to read well. Whether you are succeeding depends on whether you are meeting specific objectives for the learner. Given a dozen words he was to learn by breaking them into syllables, is he able to do it when he is finished with the meeting? Given his need to show some enthusiasm for a short story, do you note any evidence that he is interested and willing to try it again?

Another area of evaluation is the way you conduct the meeting. Are you prepared? Do you have everything organized and ready? Do you keep the session moving? If something is not working, do you change and try to reach the objective another way?

Do you prepare the next meeting by asking yourself what you need to do to move him toward his objective? If you are not making progress, or are not getting along, do you discuss it with the program director or with the child's teacher so they can advise you or give you another assignment?

Evaluation ought to be part of every meeting with the learner. Do you and the child feel successful? Are your techniques working? Are you achieving specific skills and attitude changes? If you ask these questions each time, your work should have greater direction and be more successful.

How can I teach specific reading skills? Remember the distinction between you and the classroom teacher. You do not need to be a technician. But you will need ideas and sources to work on specific reading skills. The bibliography of this book will help you with sources of published material. The teacher or program director will provide you with materials and ideas on how to proceed. Don't hesitate to ask.

A few simple guides will help you answer some of the learner's questions about pronouncing words and remembering what he has read.

Sound Guides. Vowel sounds are said to be long or short. They are long when they say their own name. The vowel "a," for example, is long in the word *made* and short in the word *mad.*

Because of certain letter combinations, the vowel may be

modified so that it is different from the short sound and the long sound. Two of the sound rules that you must know cover modified vowel sounds. The "a" in the word *car* is modified by the "r" which follows it. The vowels "o" and "i" in the word *boil* are also modified. Their separate sounds cannot be heard clearly.

Five "sound" rules will enable you to identify most of the words that you meet in your reading.

1. Short-vowel rule: When there is only one vowel in a word or syllable, that vowel usually has a short sound, if the vowel stands at the beginning or in the middle of the word; for example, *at, but*.

2. Long-vowel rule: When a two-vowel word or syllable has a silent "e" at the end, the first vowel in the word usually has a long sound; for example, *made, babe*.

3. Long-vowel rule 2: When there is a double vowel in a word or syllable, the first vowel usually has a long sound and the second vowel is silent; for example, *maid, beat*.

4. Murmur rule: When a vowel is followed by an "r" it has a modified sound that is neither characteristically long nor short; for example, *car, hurt*.

5. Diphthong rule: Certain double vowels have linked sounds that make use of both vowels; for example, the double vowel "ou" in *house*, "ew" in *new*, "ow" in *now*, "oi" in *oil*, "oy" in *boy*.

The Syllable Signal. Divide multisyllabic words into syllables and then apply the sound signal given above. Keep these guidelines in mind for syllabicating words:

1. If you hear two distinct consonant sounds between syllables, both syllables usually will be short, e.g., doctor—doc/tor. Each syllable contains the consonant-vowel-consonant arrangement, the short sound pattern.

2. If you hear only one consonant sound between syllables as in *later* and *latter*, that consonant usually will be

doubled if both syllables have a short sound, as in *latter*— lat/ter; it usually will be a single consonant if one of the syllables has a long sound, as in *later*—la/ter.

Keep in mind that the sound-spelling patterns operate on the individual syllables.

The Root-Plus Signal. You can overcome spelling difficulties by simple word analysis. Thousands of words are nothing more than a combination of a common root to which something has been added; that is, a prefix, a suffix, or an "e" ending. By breaking down a word into its parts you can get a clearer picture of its spelling, as well as its meaning.

Divide and conquer! Remember Caesar and Ben Franklin? Divide—listen for the root and additions to it; then spell— each part correctly, using the sound signals.

Here are a few simple word analyses to show you the procedure:

WORD	PREFIX	ROOT	SUFFIX OR ENDING
Meaning	_____	mean	ing
Postpone	post	pone	_____
Handful	_____	hand	ful
Premature	pre	mature	_____
Government	_____	govern	ment
Idleness	_____	idle	ness
Detour	de	tour	_____

Comprehension Guides. The key to teaching comprehension is to ask the learner the right questions. If possible, you want to keep your student thinking all the time he is reading. One way to do that is to ask four different kinds of questions after he has read a selection.

Type 1: Questions asking for details. Samples: Where did it happen? Who was there? How big was he?

Type 2: Questions asking for the main idea. Samples: What is the main idea? What was the story trying to tell us? What would be a good title for this selection?

Type 3: Questions asking for an evaluation. Samples: Was this a true story? Was the message worth anything? Did it produce the effect the author wanted it to?

Type 4: Questions asking for application. Samples: How can this information be used? Do you see a need for doing something like that? How does the story affect your life?

Teaching Specific Skills. Some specific ideas that will help you use materials from home as well as the books the teacher and the program provide are given below. These are only samples and are not meant to solve all the problems associated with teaching reading. Use them, adapt them, discard them. Judge them for your situation.

SKILL NEED	EXERCISE
Auditory Skills: Matching Rhyming Words	On the left side of the page, display pictures of objects which exemplify the sound being taught; on the right side, display pictures of rhyming words. The children are to draw a line to the rhyming object.
Auditory Skills: Identifying Consonant Sounds	Each child receives a worksheet depicting a playground scene. Most of the objects displayed in the picture start with initial consonant sounds already studied. For example, all the objects beginning with "b" are marked with a red pencil. All the objects beginning with "p" are marked with a blue pencil. Only two or three sounds should be tested at once; the picture can be used again to test other sounds.
Auditory Skills: Identifying Vowel Sounds	The children are to return to their readers to skim for words that fit into the categories given by the teacher. The categories for sorting are determined by the vowel sounds the teacher wants to stress. Exam-

SKILL NEED	EXERCISE
	ple: the long sound of *made*, the short sound of *mad*, the "r"-controlled sound of *car*.
Auditory Skills: Recognizing Number of Syllables	Give a list of mixed words containing one-, two-, and three-syllable words. The children are to unscramble the words and put them into three columns, according to the number of syllables per word. Then they are to label the columns one-, two-, and three-syllable words.
Visual Skills: Developing Special Discrimination Horizontal Sequence	Display three objects before the children and demonstrate the naming of the first, next, and last object. Using any three objects, have them locate the first, next, and last objects from left to right.
Visual Skills: Noticing Likenesses and Differences	The children are given a worksheet with pairs of similar and often confused words. As the teacher reads sentences, the children are to underline the correct word from the pair. Example: *quiet-quite, deer-dear, palace-place, throat-throne*.
Motor Skills: Developing Hand-Eye Coordination	Some developmental activities to enhance visual-motor coordination are cutting, painting, pasting, tracing, finger games, coloring, model-making, bead-stringing, and block-building.
Sight Vocabulary: Developing Sight Vocabulary	In a game played like bingo, words are written in columns and rows. The children cover the words pronounced by the teacher; the first child to completely cover a column or row is the winner.
Comprehension: Seeing Literal and Interpretive Meanings	Prepare questions to be presented to the student before he begins reading. These questions should provoke thought while reading. Some sample questions which enhance interpretation are: "What makes this a good example of _____ (some literary style)?" "What did he mean by _____?"

SKILL NEED   EXERCISE

"Do you think that this should have happened?" "Compare these two characters." "Which character displayed the most courage?" and so on.

Comprehension:
Recognizing Main
Ideas and Supporting
Detail

After the children have read the story, the teacher writes sentences on the board showing main ideas and details from the reading. Through discussion, the children distinguish which is the supporting material. Finally, each child arranges on a sheet of paper the main ideas in their proper sequence.

Comprehension:
Following Directions

Present a worksheet listing directions which vary according to topics studied in each subject for the past week. The directions are to be completed but done in fun. Some examples are: Write the page number that tells where the ants get their food. (Science.) Trace a picture of an ant. (Science.) Copy the definition of a verb. (English.)

Structural Analysis:
Recognizing Affixes

After reviewing rules about plurals, present the children with a list of representative nouns. The child is to write the root word next to the given plural, then state in his own words the rule governing that root word and its plural.

Context Clues:
Using Context Clues

Present a short story of one paragraph with some words omitted. The children are to read each sentence and complete it with their own words or those from a given list. The different types of context clues may be exhibited in each sentence.

Comprehension:
Definitions and Word
Symbols

Prepare a worksheet of words and definitions which the children must match up. The choice of words and definitions depends on the grade level of the group Give an example of a verb used in a sentence. (English.) From your notebook, copy three new words learned this week in Spanish. Draw a Pilgrim boy or girl. (Social Studies.) State three reasons why we still observe Thanksgiving. (Social Studies.) Spell correctly three words that you missed on the pretest. (Spelling.)

Comprehension Rate: Scanning

Questions involving material found in the index, table of contents, and chapter headings make good material for scanning exercises.

Oral Reading Skills: Enunciating Correctly

Bring attention to endings like -ing, -d, and -t. Practice words on flashcards can be used for individual or class help:

chattering	brought	quiet
coming	feed	slid
fishing	dived	caught
talking	crept	carried
stirring	spent	tonight
falling	listened	right
blowing	chattered	around
making	watched	tugged
growling	rattled	that
pushing	waited	pulled

Interest and Attitudes. To keep the attention and interest of the learner you must know something about his interests and attitudes. His parents and teachers can help you list his interests and let you know what he says about school, reading, and other aspects of his life. The learner himself will probably tell you directly or indirectly many of the same things, so listen and watch. As much as possible, do not ask him to fill out forms or tests to reveal his interests. Talk to him about books and school and work, ask him what appeals to him. With that information, you can select materials, develop exercises, plan field trips, or develop your own knowledge so you have something to talk about. It will help if you use things he will enjoy while working on the reading problem. If he likes to build models, for example, use the words on some of the boxes to develop sight words and to practice word-analysis skills—an excellent combination of interest and skill development.

Get On with It. Tips for reading and working with youngsters who need help are endless. You now have sufficient knowledge to begin with confidence. If you need or want additional knowledge, there are books suggested in the bibliography that can help. The point is that you can make an important contribution to a learner's skill and to his life by encouraging him and guiding him through some simple practices. You are not expected to be the expert—and that is your strength in the tutor-learner relationship.

7 ❧ Recommendations

O NE PERSON counts, but no man is an island (or an Atlas), and the key to effective volunteer action, as in so many other social enterprises, is the engineering of assent and collaboration.

Our visits and surveys of programs across the country make us confident that the lay person *can* contribute to the improvement of literacy in the United States, both through direct, personal involvement and by acting as a catalyst in motivating and recruiting others to the cause. It is clear that volunteers offer classroom teachers extra hands and eyes; meet children on a personal basis and thereby expand the self-esteem of some of them; and work with adults under circumstances that do not seem threatening or patronizing to those who have not learned to read adequately. Despite some obvious draw-backs—many learners, young and old, may not have access to the kinds of instruction and materials they need—the millions of volunteers who can work to improve literacy multiply immeasurably the human and material resources which we have available to try to solve this persistent social problem.

We offer these recommendations to assist the development and expansion of volunteer forces in the field of reading.

First, a few general guidelines covering the community:

A. *A community-wide inventory of reading needs and resources.* The following community reading inventory model is drawn from "Sound and Light for the Right to Read," a multimedia kit prepared by Virginia Mathews for the National Book Committee.

A well-planned program of reading development needs to begin with knowing where to start. What is the size and shape of the reading problem in your community, be it town or city, county school district or state?

In general, it is useful to know or to find out through surveys, interviews, and facts gathered from a variety of sources something about: (1) the present status and level of reading efficiency among both children and adults, and (2) what reading resources are available in the community, including both instructional programs and materials.

Remember that when you seek improvements in the implementation of the community's Right to Read there are going to be—there should be—people who want to know why improvements are necessary. Among the skeptics and the challengers, if your efforts are successful, will be influential authority figures from the political, economic, and educational leadership as well as newspapers, civic groups, parents, and taxpayers. You will need to have facts to show them that what exists in the way of resources does not provide the Right to Read in all its aspects for all the children or adults in the community.

In trying to assess the literacy level or reading efficiency level of the community, it is important to get points of view and facts from diverse sources, outside of the schools as well as within them. It may be that certain professionals within the school systems have developed a greater tolerance for reading failure than is acceptable to the work world outside the school. Sights and expectations can be raised by unaccustomed dialogues between reading teachers, supervisors and other school people, and employers and personnel workers. These are, of course, delicate matters and inquiries; sharing and pooling of viewpoints must be carried out with the utmost tact and care, so that everyone understands that the whole Right to Read effort must be carried out through collaboration between the schools and all concerned public and private segments of the community. It is most important to emphasize and reemphasize that the total community shares the responsibility for whatever has gone wrong; it is not the fault of the schools alone, or a particular instructional method that they may or may not have been using. In other words, "The name of the game is sharing the blame and erasing the shame!" While there may be enormous sensitivity to inventory, measurement, comparisons, ratings, and accountability, in general much of the problem is a "hidden" one. Not all of the following may be applicable to every situation, but here are some general directions for questions to which you may want answers:

1. What percentage of the community's adults—over eighteen years of age—can be classified as illiterate or functionally illiterate; that is, disabled on the job or in life situations by reading deficiency?

2. What percentage of the secondary-school students—junior high and high school—are having difficulty because of reading problems?

3. What percentage of the community- or junior-college or technical-school students are in trouble because of reading problems?

4. What is the dropout rate from junior high and high school? In what percentage of these cases do principals and other school officials estimate that reading failure is a factor?

5. What relationship between crime patterns and illiteracy has been observed by police and court officials?

6. Get points of view about the overall and specific read-

ing competence of persons in your community from such people as, for instance: welfare workers; the personnel director of a local plant; a newspaper reporter; the state employment service branch; the local bureau of motor vehicles. If some of the people with whom the above come in contact do not appear to be functional readers and thinkers, what do they think is the reason for this deficiency?

7. Be sure to talk with all of the types of professional people in the schools who deal with reading, especially reading specialists and librarians, but also curriculum planners and principals, subject supervisors and classroom teachers in the primary grades. Get their slant on what they think they are doing well or poorly, what factors are limiting their best efforts, and what improvements could be made.

8. Check out, at least on a spot-check basis, newspaper subscriptions; newsstand and paperback rack sales; magazine subscriptions; library cards held and their frequency of use; bookstore sales. Do residents of certain neighborhoods, students or graduates of certain schools, appear to read more, and with more satisfaction, than others?

9. What requirements are made of elementary-school teachers concerning their knowledge of how to teach reading and how to select and use a great variety of books and other materials in the classroom?

10. Do your schools have reading specialists on the staff? Do they work with and through the classroom teachers as well as directly with children who have reading problems? Do they keep teachers updated by means of additional on-the-job training? Do they work after school, or on free time during the day, or when?

11. What is the diagnostic and prescriptive process in reading instruction for all children entering school? What is the referral process for children who seem to be having trouble? How is instruction handled during the school day?

12. What individual attention from subject teachers and reading specialists is available to junior-high and high-school students?

13. What can you find about the community's preschool programs in terms of their concerted development of prereading skills? Make a check of kindergarten, prekindergarten, nursery-school, day-care, Head Start, and other programs, both public and private, to see what is going on in terms of developing verbal skills, recognition of letters, sounds, colors, shapes, numbers, and other conceptual and reasoning skills.

14. Is there any parent training going on in support of reading and prereading skills, especially among the parents of preschool and elementary-school children?

15. What kinds of outside-of-school or informal school-related tutoring or motivation programs are going on? Who is involved? Who is training these helpers, and with what goals in mind? Is there any systematic evaluation of the training programs and the volunteers' performance?

16. What kinds of reading programs are available for out-of-school young adults and adults in the community (over eighteen): Public-high-school adult-education classes? Private reading clinics? Industry-sponsored programs? Programs and classes in other agencies, such as public libraries?

17. How extensive are the book-ownership resources of the community? Are there bookstores with wide selections beyond current bestsellers? Conveniently located paperback bookstores, newsstands and stationery stores with good general "backlist" stocks?

18. Most important, how extensive, how interconnected and accessible are the libraries available to community residents? Are public-library outlets—branches, stations, bookmobiles—located where people live and work? Do locations move and change to keep up with user needs? Do open hours include some nights, Saturdays, Sundays? Is there a minimum

of rules, restrictions, and red tape set up between the library's books and other materials and those who would use them? Does organization of print and nonprint materials make sense to the nonspecialist user?

19. Does each school building in the community have a centralized library-media center with supply lines into every part of the school building? Is use of the center restricted by hours open, public schedule, shortage of staff? Are the services of a qualified professional library-media specialist available to all children enrolled in the schools, including kindergarten and preschool programs? Are qualified school-library-media specialists supported by clerical and semiprofessional staff and services such as centralized processing? Do teachers receive constant in-service support from library staff members, and are library staff members involved in all instructional program planning?

20. Does each institution of higher education or adult education in the community have its own planned and formalized library service component which has responsibility for supporting the work of its students? Adult evening classes? Basic-adult-education classes? Technical school? Extension class of the college? Are instructors aware that they must supply, through their methods of instruction, most of the impetus for reading-habit formation and practice?

21. Are library programs and services available to community residents that will motivate them to read and help develop a reading climate in the community? Are these programs and services available without great effort or special knowledge? Are they available through other agencies—hospitals, day-care centers, senior-citizen and community and neighborhood centers—as well as directly on the streets, in the parks, and in library buildings?

B. *Training for professionals (teachers and librarians) who are to work with volunteers is essential for effective pro-*

grams. There should be a multidisciplinary approach to training; i.e., teachers, librarians, and others should be involved in training sessions.

C. *Multiagency auspices are desirable for volunteer projects;* i.e., collaboration between the school or public-library system with community action and other social agencies, with other community-serving institutions and the private sector.

D. *Evaluations—successes and failures—should be given broadly effective dissemination.* "Communications" in an agency budget should be a large enough item to cover more than postage and telephone calls; in the absence of any formal network for the circulation and exchange of information, local and state agencies and programs should ensure their own, informal channels of cross-communication.

Here are some specific action recommendations at varying operational levels:

LOCAL SCHOOLS

1. *All school districts should implement volunteer reading programs.* Visible benefits are enthusiasm among children, a sense of community involvement, and an awareness in the school of the need for human contact in learning.

2. *Establish inexpensive summer reading programs staffed primarily by volunteers.* The purpose is to maintain the achieved skills and to prevent a regression or a lack of interest.

3. *Use volunteer groups in the neighborhood to help identify language differences or other environmental factors that might interfere with reading.* These people can act as census takers for the school or as salesmen to encourage parents to let the school know their wishes about education. Volunteers can help the teacher collect information about the children in the classroom. By using checklists or other information-

gathering devices the teacher can ask the volunteer to see each child individually and then compile a class profile.

STATE AND LOCAL GOVERNMENT

4. *Regional conferences should be held to enable volunteers to share ideas and to coordinate efforts among different programs.*

5. *Conduct training programs for volunteers over radio and educational television.* Printed material could be prepared for these programs so that the prospective volunteer has reading and practice material to match the messages over the airwaves. Radio and TV can also be used to publicize volunteer efforts in reading. Many cities now require CATV franchisers to devote a specified number of hours for educational purposes.

FEDERAL GOVERNMENT

6. *One or more evaluation plans should be developed and distributed to assist volunteer projects.* The federal government should also be interested in the effectiveness of volunteer programs in order to give guidelines to those groups interested in establishing them.

7. *Training programs for volunteers in reading should be developed and packaged for easy distribution.* Because the layman often has little or no technical knowledge, help is needed in training efforts. The U.S. Office of Education could prepare and distribute training packages.

8. *Conduct research on the effects of using neighborhood help to change the behavior of poverty children with reading difficulties.* The recommendation has special significance where

dialect may make a difference in understanding the language of the school.

9. *Conduct research on the effect of a volunteer in the classroom on the behavior of the teacher.* Some observers believe that the presence of another adult in the classroom causes increased alertness and professional activity by the teacher.

10. *Recruit volunteers by advertising and program development.* The Office of Voluntary Action, local libraries and schools may be focal points to spearhead recruitment.

11. *Volunteer service to education ought to be made an acceptable substitute for military service.* Benefits to the nation and to the individual would be similar to those received by their participation in the military, that is, protection of rights (right to learn), and sense of commitment to national goals.

12. *Time, facilities, and materials donated to volunteer programs should be tax-deductible.*

13. *Conduct research on the kinds of tasks, techniques, and materials that are used most effectively by laymen.* For example, should they use materials that are known and available—materials such as magazines, newspapers, and fliers?

LIBRARIES

14. *Concerned agencies should consider cooperative programs that will enable the entire family to receive benefits of the reading effort.* Libraries, for example, could include a day-care center and an adult storytelling operation at the same time that special reading instruction takes place.

15. *Libraries should develop a program of going into the community to interest unreached people in the world of books.* Bookmobiles, delivery carts, playground programs, and so on, are ways of beginning extended library activity.

VARIOUS GROUPS

16. *Colleges should provide special courses for volunteers in reading programs.*

17. *Colleges should also use teacher-intern programs as a means of providing volunteer services to youngsters in school.*

18. *Senior-citizen centers and groups should organize tutor activities for neighborhood children.*

19. *The use of the handicapped and youth tutoring youth should be encouraged.*

20. *Redirect VISTA-like programs to feed specifically into educational programs.* Training and structure can be provided for these young volunteers.

21. *Both cognitive and affective goals should be incorporated into tutorial programs.* Since tutoring affects both skills and attitudes, then tutors should attempt to treat both.

22. *Television and newspapers should consider carrying reading instruction on a regular basis for skill development and basic literacy training.*

23. *Labor unions, businesses, fraternal organizations, etc., should use some of their resources to set up volunteer reading programs.*

24. *Communities should pay people to open their homes for study hour or open storefront study halls to provide reading opportunity and service to youth.*

25. *Businesses should be encouraged, perhaps through tax benefits, to release employees for a few hours a week to work as volunteers in reading programs sponsored by schools and libraries in the community.*

wanted to educate themselves. Libraries thus geared themselves to help the person who came to the library. Today many libraries take an active role in promoting literacy and in teaching people to read. They have devised creative and exciting ways of motivating and teaching. This reflects a broadening objective of the typical public library. It is moving out of its central walls and into a variety of neighborhood locations, using many vehicles for reaching the neighborhoods. In fact, it is reaching patrons who weren't aware they had an interest in the library and a need for it.

The librarian and the volunteers in library programs are not certified reading or classroom teachers, but they have joined a host of other noncertified teachers in attempting to overcome reading problems and in motivating reluctant readers to expand their interests and skills.

For different libraries there may be different target audiences. Some are concerned with preschool programs, others with reaching disadvantaged youngsters, others with adult literacy. To contact these people and to lure them into the library, many techniques are being tried. There are libraries sending high-school students into poverty neighborhoods with grocery carts stacked with books. Like old-time street hawkers, they gather interested customers and give them books. Those who take books are asked to return them to the cart the following week. But no records are kept or fines imposed. When someone returns a book, he exchanges it for a new one. Door-to-door storytellers, traveling puppet shows, preschool story hours in neighborhood community centers, and family programs are supplemented with books, films, slides, posters, and records to show the scope of the library.

Librarians and their assistants use basic learning principles in their programs: (1) to get the reader used to reading, start with his interests; (2) show him how attractive and how enjoyable reading can be; (3) provide him with books appropriate to his level; (4) use a vocabulary he can understand; (5)

help him relate a book to his own experience; (6) challenge him to grow; and (7) praise and encourage him every step of the way.

Those are guidelines everyone can follow. With that attitude, librarians and library volunteers contribute to literacy even though they are not conducting technical classes in specific reading skills, and they demonstrate that books can be exciting and valuable.

Before a library decides on how it is going to reach out, it has to determine who it is reaching for. Once the audience for the service has been established, then the storytellers, the buses, the carts, and the book racks can be obtained and the service advertised. From what we have seen, some libraries focus on a specific age group, some on those with specific characteristics, some on the family. In the section that follows, there are hints as to how some libraries reach their patrons *directly* once they have identified them.

The Prince George County, Maryland, Library sent a librarian through one community ringing a cow bell to attract listeners to storytime. Children flocked around, heard a story, and learned about other library services.

A storytelling festival was held to celebrate United Nations Day, in a tentlike enclosure on the mall of a shopping plaza. Ten storytellers appeared in the native dress of countries represented by their stories.

The library showed films on the side of a mini-bus, sponsored book-oriented programs on television, and produced miniature theaters (based on the English penny theaters)—all designed to promote reading as a by-product of the literary-theatrical approach. Workshops were held for children to learn about puppetry through live demonstrations and films. Children created characters and stories from their own imagination and produced shows. Reading was reinforced when they turned to existing stories for ideas and situations.

Bivens Memorial Library, Amarillo, Texas, gives special

attention to two Mexican-American communities through bookmobile stops at their CAP community centers, offering individual readers guidance and storytelling at both centers as well as maintaining a large stock of books in Spanish.

The Public Library of Cincinnati and Hamilton County, Cincinnati, Ohio. A joint project which was begun during the summer of 1969 between the Public Recreation Commission and the Public Library of Cincinnati was continued with the assistance of federal funding, which provided for two play-mobiles to visit informal play areas with a driver and a student librarian. The Recreation Commission added enough federal funds so that five playmobiles could be sent out, each with two students as staff.

Inside the vans are play equipment, games, craft materials to be used in areas where there is no staffed playground—on vacant lots, blocked-off streets, etc. To this the library added paperbacks, a work table, and display racks. Staff was given training by the Recreation Commission and the library.

The paperbacks were selected with an eye to sixteen-year-olds, but the patrons actually using the collection turned out to be mostly between the ages of six and twelve, with a scattering of young adults. Since 99 percent of the areas visited were black, the materials leaned heavily on black literature. However, *Curious George*, the Dr. Seuss books, and any title by Zim were the most popular.

The Division of Library Services for the Hawaii State Department of Education has centered its attention on two outreach programs: (1) the implementation of Japanese-language materials—circulation and reporting mechanisms; and (2) the utilization of library materials for the disadvantaged, mainly for the preschool and primary levels.

Because of the inclusion of these Japanese-language materials, libraries throughout the state began to serve this ethnic group in many instances for the first time. Materials for the disadvantaged were offered to community agencies without the customary restrictions of fines and/or fees for lost materials.

The Indianapolis–Marion County Public Library, Indianapolis, Indiana, cooperates with Flanner House, a neighborhood program, in a storefront library that is open weekday afternoons. It serves a housing project near a hospital, mostly with children's activities. The juvenile detention center requested library aid in a weekly program for children age six to eighteen who are minor offenders or victims of parental neglect. One part of their program is for dropouts and the other helps the inmates keep up with their regular schoolwork. Boys and girls have come into the library after their release.

The Lansing, Michigan, Public Library has an adult-education program sponsored jointly by the school system. The following considerations were kept in mind in selecting books: reading level, one to eight; minority considerations; paperbacks, for their low cost and "friendliness"; broad range of subjects; strict GED goal-oriented material; homemaking and craft books for mothers' clubs; Spanish-language material.

The Long Beach, California, Public Library. Among its outreach programs, Long Beach participated in selecting and delivering books and films to programs sponsored by the city recreation department. All the teen posts operated under the local CAP agency receive paperback discards from the library. Paperback racks, donated by local vendors, were installed in all of them. Through continuing contact with the teen post directors, the book racks are kept supplied with books that appeal to the teens.

Recognizing the cultural needs of the minority groups in Long Beach, the library developed special collections of books for Japanese- and Spanish-speaking people, among others. An effort was made to gather popular books in these collections to encourage the young people to use the library.

The Milwaukee, Wisconsin, Public Library issues a *Community Newsletter*, published by the Adult Basic Education and Community Librarian projects. It is written by community people (with some articles in Spanish) as a medium for communication about inner-city problems and where to find help for them.

The Norfolk, Virginia, Public Library System gives story hours, singly or in series, for children from preschool through sixth grade at approximately ten public and private elementary schools; at the recreation centers connected with the Norfolk Redevelopment and Housing Authority; at six STOP Child Development Centers; at the Colonial Avenue Boys' Club; at the Barraud Park STOP Day Camp; and at the King's Daughters Children's Hospital.

Other activities for children included: "Doorstep Storytelling" by personnel from two branches, nature talks in neighboring kindergartens by one branch, and a series of book talks at an elementary school.

The Oklahoma City–County Libraries. The staff took books and films to the County Homes for boys and girls who are wards of the court, to the Juvenile Detention Home, and to a home for unwed mothers. High-interest paperbacks such as science fiction, books on dating and grooming, and mystery stories were distributed. High-interest magazines such as *Hot Rod, American Girl,* and *Seventeen* proved to be an excellent bridge to the reading experience for many of these young people.

The Free Library of Philadelphia, Pennsylvania, developed a demonstration reading program to reach and help the culturally disadvantaged. Three main objectives were to make materials available to meet the various needs of young adults and adults whose reading level is eighth grade or below; to provide and encourage the use of helpful materials for nonreaders who have the ability to read; and to provide various means of interesting young children in reading.

Nearly all the book material was in paperback, and multiple copies were available for loan to various agencies as well as individuals. Four full-time librarians and several staff members guided various aspects of the program.

A creative dramatics program was set up to motivate children and their families to use libraries and books. Parents served as aides on trips, made simple props, and attended classes when invited. A creative-dramatics leader spent two days a week on the bookmobiles and two days in branches (Vacation Reading Club meetings) telling stories, showing films, and leading creative-dramatics sessions.

For several years the Office of Work with Children sent a librarian to the Youth Study Center, a detention center for children (ages eight to seventeen) under the jurisdiction of the county court, for a weekly story-hour program. The story hours were for the younger boys and girls in their living unit. The books were left for a two-week period, and when the librarian returned, they asked her questions or made comments about plot, characters, and endings of the books.

The Multnomah County Library, Portland, Oregon. Over one hundred volunteers from local churches assisted teachers in the schools and tried to blanket certain districts with books by placing them in social-service agencies, day-care centers, waiting rooms, neighborhood centers—anyplace a child might be. Directors of neighborhood centers were encouraged to give a child a book to take home and keep for his own. Paperback books were given to migrant families, and "Sesame Street" booklists were mimeographed and distributed.

The Wake County Public Libraries, Raleigh, North Carolina. Two branch libraries are used to hold adult reading classes. They have developed a small collection of low-reading-level/high-interest children's books without the stigma of the traditional "j" on the spines. Summer workshops for children enabled them to make their own hand-drawn 16-mm films which became part of the library's film collection. They are often borrowed for Parent Nights and other group programs. "There seems to be no special rural-city or black-white division as to which books are read most. Almost all children like those books and stories that an enthusiastic adult has introduced to them."

The St. Paul, Minnesota, Public Library. Regular programs during the school year at Boys Totem Town, a juvenile detention home in St. Paul, bring the library to a group whose energies might be challenged through ideas from books. The program, held one night a week, was staffed by one librarian, who was assisted by a staff member working part-time at the library and the home. Each program featured a speaker or a discussion of a specific subject with the librarian supporting the discussion with books related to the subject. Occasionally the program would consist of book talks or just open discussions. The bulk of the books brought along by the librarian for the boys to check out were paperbacks, popular titles.

The Scranton, Pennsylvania, Public Library. The "Lookie Bookie" goes wherever teen-agers are, showing library films and lending paperback books at its afternoon and evening stops throughout the city. "Lookie Bookie" was the brainchild of Sumner White, director of the Scranton Public Library, and Anthony Musso, coordinator for the Title I federal funds and instructional materials for the Scranton School District.

A grant of $6,000 enabled "Lookie Bookie" to roll out of the library's parking lot and carry its sights and sounds to the city's teen-agers at such locations as Connell Park, Adams School Playground, Bellevue Community Center, Hilltop Manor, Jackson Street Playground, Tripp Park, Nay Aug Park, and many other neighborhoods.

Loudspeakers mounted on the van roof heralded its arrival, as the latest in pop music told the neighborhood that "Lookie Bookie" is back once again. The crew would set up book display racks and at the nearest house would ask permission to use an electrical outlet to operate the movie projector. After giving people time to select their books and magazines, the movie would be shown, and several films would fill the next hour or two. Crowds of over seventy-five persons have attended the evening showings, even when there was little or no advance notice.

In its first four weeks, "Lookie Bookie" attracted over two thousand Scrantonians of all ages. While books and films were selected with the interest of teen-agers in mind, the selection of books was broadened to include some titles for adults as well, but the primary purpose remained to find out what teen-agers want to read, and what they want to view on film.

The Wheeler, Alabama, Regional Library. All Head Start children visited the library for instruction and orientation in library usage. They also had a story hour.

A tutorial service in a branch of Wheeler Basin Regional Library was begun to help any student who needed assistance with homework. This was staffed by high-school students organized by the First United Methodist Church. The study center was located in the Community Room of a housing project whose population is predominantly black. The center was managed by volunteers (two men and two women), including at least one teacher, and other adults interested in helping children. The librarian supplied an encyclopedia, a dictionary, and other study aids, as well as newspapers and magazines.

Books were also sent to start a library in a recently constructed high-rise apartment building for elderly people with low incomes. A tenant in the apartment opened the library each day.

The Yonkers, New York, Public Library. Workshops in storytelling, puppetry, music, and dramatics have been held, as was Project SOAR (Summer Opportunity for Art and Reading). The library sponsored the reading part, while the Hudson River Museum sponsored the art program. The library toured the inner city with a mini-mobile and bussed the participants to the nearest library for further exposure to reading.

The Hutchinson, Kansas, Public Library. This center for the South Central Kansas Library System initiated a practical approach to library service for rural readers, a library-by-mail program designed to provide current, popular reading in paperback form to the residents of an eleven-county region. The library continuously builds a mailing list (approaching 25,000 names) of people who would like to receive books by mail. People make a selection by mail, receive their book by mail, and send it back in a special mailer provided by the library. The library staff developed a catalog of approximately one thousand titles, which is mailed to rural residents. Included is an order blank that can accommodate eight selections. A patron selects titles by marking the order blank and sends the postage-paid form to the library. The books are lent for a period of three weeks.

The overdue-book problem is handled without fines. Patrons are urged to read the books, return them when finished, and not worry about fines. The loss of a book (about forty cents for most paperbacks) is preferred by the library to the loss of a patron. The 90-percent return rate (considering loss in mail, loss in homes, damaged books, etc.) was not worse than the loss-and-theft rate of over-the-counter lending.

In a random survey of the patrons using the service, the library staff found that many current users were former nonusers.

The Monmouth County, New Jersey, Public Library. One of the ways the library tried to have an impact on disadvantaged communities in the county was via storytellers going from door to door to invite children to a story hour and to give them a sample of what they would hear. The storytelling program was conducted throughout the system. This campaign recruited, trained, and dispatched the storytellers.

Suspicious parents and shy children were won over by their enthusiasm. Neighborhood teen-agers, used as aides in the library program, helped to make this an especially attractive idea for the community.

The Monmouth County, Alabama, Library spread its influence by utilizing a storymobile in rural areas, films and filmstrips, free paperbacks, and small neighborhood-library units. Its bookmobile service operated on a twelve-to-fourteen-hour-a-day schedule. Mornings were reserved for neighborhood service for preschoolers and their parents in story hours. Afternoons went to school-age children and adults, with paperback collections as the attraction. Registration cards, parents' permission, and fines for overdue books were not required. In the evening the bookmobile visited rural communities and showed films of both juvenile and adult interest.

The Atlanta, Georgia, Public Library. One of its efforts was appropriately called Project BAIT (Books of Absorbing Interest—Televised). Funded through Title III of the Library Services and Construction Act, BAIT is a cooperative program with the Atlanta and Fulton County school systems and the educational TV station, WETV, operated by the city. Twelve fifteen-minute TV programs were produced by WETV. The purpose of the series was to present books in an appealing manner, to help deepen the appreciation of good literature, stimulate more children and young people to read books of value, and contribute to the cultural development of the underprivileged. An outstanding children's book was filmed for each program. Films are housed in the library and are lent to educational TV stations, libraries, and schools throughout the Southeast.

Through a grant from the National Endowment for the Arts, co-sponsored by the Atlanta Public Library and the Georgia Commission on the Arts, Project Enlarge was formed in June, 1968, as part of the Urban Mythology Film Program.

It started with a group of twenty-four teen-agers from the southeast section of Atlanta. They conceived situations to show through filmmaking the interaction between the human psyche and its environment.

More than one hundred teen-agers have participated in the program, in which they learned to operate cameras and light meters, develop their film, enlarge their prints, and think up situations to photograph. Several of the teen-agers have won awards in national photography shows. A traveling exhibit from Project Enlarge called "Shoot the Bones" was shown in major cities throughout the United States.

The Atlanta library is also investigating other ways to reach the disadvantaged. One is a locally sponsored commercial TV show for children. Another is a cooperative program with Academy Theater, a local community group which has actors in residence in the Atlanta public school system. Branch librarians help the actors to interact with children from the neighborhoods.

We are also citing a few of the many possible examples of the *indirect* service approach, when libraries help volunteers establish rapport with the people they, in turn, want to reach.

Storytelling, long a favorite library activity, compares well in competition with other visual presentations. Storytelling with illustrations has almost as much fascination for children and adults as a movie version of the book.

The Philadelphia Free Library sends out storytellers to schools, settlement houses, parks, playgrounds, hospitals, churches, camps, street corners, etc., for preschool through eighth-grade listeners. The training of storytellers becomes a part of spreading the image of the library as a lively place. The Philadelphia library conducted workshops and training sessions regularly.

Teachers, teacher aides, and parents have been trained in

the selection of books and in techniques of reading aloud. A psychologist at the Hahnemann Hospital Mental Health Clinic asked the cooperation of the Free Library in a project to train ghetto mothers with limited reading ability to read picture books to their children. The purpose of the project was to develop the quality of the mothers' reading ability and at the same time to give the children an introduction to good books. A librarian trained the mothers in book selection and reading aloud. Later on, these mothers began to teach other mothers and children.

A storytelling workshop of eight three-hour sessions was held at four agencies of the Free Public Library, in four areas of the city, for public and parochial-school librarians and library aides.

The Norfolk, Virginia, Public Library completed a storytelling workshop for Norfolk junior-high-school students selected by the Volunteer Service Bureau. The training included instruction in how to conduct picture-book programs for preschoolers, how to tell stories to school-age children, how to select good stories and picture books for telling, and how to plan a well-balanced story program. Each student had practice in presenting picture books and in telling a ten-to-fifteen-minute-long folk tale before the workshop group. Part of the training included observing experienced storytellers.

Augusta–Richmond County Public Library, Augusta, Georgia, conducted book-centered discussion groups with Upward Bound students at Paine College, and demonstrations in storytelling to leaders of day-care centers and kindergarten teachers.

Okefenokee Regional Library, Waycross, Georgia, established a corps of storytellers to work through the schools in a rural section. The library has conducted numerous storytelling workshops or training sessions for adults. The most ambitious of these to date was an all-day workshop, open to anyone desiring to attend. One hundred and thirty came, from seventeen counties, representing numerous interests: teachers; school and public librarians; workers from centers for exceptional children; Scouts; Sunday-school workers; representatives of library boards, kindergartens, and nurseries; workers with the disadvantaged; and interested parents.

Louisville Free Public Library, Louisville, Kentucky, conducted several storytelling workshops for Head Start teachers and their aides. The workshops, presented each fall, with separate sessions for each group, were held in the library. Book collections were available to Head Start teachers for a circulation period of eight weeks. A librarian has been part of the formal training sessions for Head Start teachers, lecturing about children's books, introducing picture books and poetry to children, and demonstrating storytelling.

The St. Paul, Minnesota, Public Library serves volunteers (as part of its family-involvement plan) with puppetry workshops for Scouts and other teen-agers working with children. Storytelling techniques are also part of these workshops.

"Getting to the people" is the emphasis of many of today's public libraries. To improve and sustain reading, books have to be available. Some people need to be convinced, however, that there are books for them. How libraries reach out is probably not as important as the fact that they decided to do so and contacted various groups to get the job done.

For many libraries an effort to reach out may be foreign to their philosophy. In interviews with many librarians, even some who were engaged in such activities, they expressed the conflicts libraries are having in acting as a pumping station instead of a reservoir. A library can be both, of course. It can be the central storehouse of books and services for those who come to it to educate themselves, and it can pump ideas and books into the communities by the means we have described here. No one can decide for a library whether it will take on a more aggressive social-action function. Each staff will have to wrestle with that decision. But the opportunity is there for those who agree to help the poor, the disenchanted, and the illiterate.

READING IS FUN-DAMENTAL PROGRAMS

The District of Columbia Public Schools. A proposal to use Title I funds for a paperback program in the elementary schools resulted in the distribution of 60,000 books to thirty-four schools by RIF, paid for by $30,000 from Title I funds.

RIF encourages other groups to help by matching their funds. Any community group that wants to purchase RIF books will receive a matching amount of books from RIF.

Requests for books to be delivered to D.C. inner-city churches have increased. Through suggestions and help from RIF coordinators, Church Women United are using them effectively in such programs as preschool groups, boys' clubs, girls' clubs, teen-age black-history study groups, and day-care centers that are housed in churches.

At irregular intervals through the year RIF received a check from Father Ray Malmonson, the Catholic chaplain at the Lorton Reformatory. The funds are provided by groups and friends as well as by some of the departing inmates who have enjoyed the books RIF has supplied for Father Ray's library.

Father Ray developed the library because the library at Lorton did not have books of interest to the men. He set up an honor system of checking out RIF books and had excellent response. The books became very popular and increasingly in demand.

Father Ray relayed a letter from the head of the Lorton library with a list of RIF-type books, requesting an estimate of the cost for the number of paperbacks listed. Soon after, RIF received a check for the total amount, and the books were picked up by Father Ray for delivery to the library.

The Youth Serving Youth Project is operated by the Pupil Personnel Technician-Aide Title I Team of the D.C. public schools in collaboration with the Neighborhood Youth Corps. This project employs Neighborhood Youth Corps enrollees to help younger pupils develop their communication skills and gain self-confidence and a positive self-image.

During the first year of the program they had no funds for books for the tutors who worked on a one-to-one basis. RIF supplied books for the program during this time. Subsequently, they received a relatively small allotment—about $1,000—to purchase books, which RIF matched.

The Women's Board of Children's Hospital approved the expenditure of funds for books to be matched by RIF. The books are used by volunteers and the nursing staff. Frequently the children keep them. The books are put in all waiting rooms and are considered expendable. The supply is replenished as the books disappear. Both children and parents have responded enthusiastically to the books.

The hospital's volunteer corps was inspired to start a story-reading and storytelling instruction course for their volunteers, and the enrollment was so large that the course had to be given a second time.

Funds for a pilot-model day-care center in Anacostia have been given by the Junior League and to the National Capital Area Child Day Care Association. A portion of these funds has been allotted to match RIF's to purchase books for the pilot center.

RIF-Funded Books to Meet Community Needs. During the summer, in addition to the bookmobile lending program, RIF books are given to about a dozen underfunded summer programs in housing projects, recreation centers, neighborhood centers, etc. Three divisions of public welfare and the children and youth centers at Laurel have been recipients of RIF books.

RIF has given books to a tutoring center an ex-teacher set up in her home. Without funding, she operates a program five days a week after school for about fifty children each day. Children come from the neighborhood and from as far away as the area around Tubman School. Tutors come from high schools in Montgomery County, Trinity College, and Augustina and Carmelite seminaries, and they are supervised by young seminarians and graduate students.

Book distributions have also been made to the Community Laundry, Twelfth Place Community Center, Receiving Home, Garfield Terrace Community Center, Montana Recreation Center, Adams-Morgan Community Center, West Potomac Public Housing Multi-Service Center, and Sibley Plaza Housing. Books were sent to the Savoy School Library, a new school which had not received funds for library books for last year.

Sale of Books. RIF has been one of the sponsors of a Black Arts and Book Fair as part of the Capitol East Community Organization's CECO EXPO 70 celebration. The D.C. Public Library and the D.C. Commission of the Arts also sponsored the fair.

RIF supplied the books for sale at the fair. Profits from the sales went to Community Laundries, Inc., which planned to set up a book-selling operation with RIF's assistance in their community room. Black people in Washington find there are few stores that sell black-oriented books, especially for children of elementary-school age.

RIF in Cleveland. "You mean I can keep it?" cries a seven-year-old child as he clutches a book he has just chosen at a book fair sponsored by RIF in Cleveland, Ohio. Another youngster approaches the table where a wide variety of colorful books are displayed and exclaims, "I can pick any book I want. My teacher told me!" These are the cries of excited children who for many reasons have not entered the mainstream of American life where the opportunity to develop close relationships with books and other reading material is usually taken for granted.

Cleveland was the second city to develop RIF programs. A cooperative relationship with the Cleveland public schools made it possible to conduct the program in schools receiving Title I funding. Although the RIF staff recognized schools as an excellent way to distribute books to deprived children, it also appreciated the fact that other informal places could likewise serve as invaluable distribution points. Accordingly, book distributions were planned in cooperation with tutorial and community centers, libraries, and detention homes.

While methods and procedures for book distribution vary, they do seem to follow a general pattern. They take the form of a book fair. Each book fair consists of a predistribution meeting followed by the actual display and selection of books. The predistribution session is usually an assembly during which the recipients stage a program. The youngsters engage in such activities as pantomime, acting, puppeteering, etc. All assemblies have one thing in common—to promote the coming of RIF. Moreover, numerous colorful posters depicting the "reading-can-be-fun" theme decorate the walls of classrooms and corridors. Teachers, librarians, parents, and children work together in implementing these predistribution programs. Effort is made to involve as many parents as possible.

On the same day as the predistribution assembly or on the following day, the children select books. The books are usually displayed on tables in primary- and intermediate-grade categories in order to guide children. Although some are confused at first by the sight of so many different kinds of books, most youngsters come to the distributions eager to select a book of their own. Indeed, it is heart-warming and at times overwhelming to observe these children as they learn to make friends with books.

The RIF program operates on the firm belief that children feel strongly about choosing the books they want to read. Something of each child goes into the selection of a book—that something is unique and the product of the child's individuality. While visiting a book fair at one of the local inner-city schools, a Cleveland industrialist noticed one youngster choose two books which he felt were obviously beyond the child's reading ability. Admitting with some hindsight that he had violated the spirit of RIF, the gentleman suggested to the child that the chosen books might be too difficult to read. The youngster indignantly informed him that he didn't think they were too difficult. "Besides," the boy said, "they are my books!" The implication was that the child chose them and would find a way to learn what was in them.

The problem arises as to what extent children should be helped in selecting books. Every effort is made to direct pupils to books of suitable grade level and possible interest, but teachers are discouraged from telling a child that he has chosen a book that is too difficult. The emphasis is on fun! And there is no attempt to equate books with children's instructional levels. RIF attempts to make reading pleasurable.

Appendix B ❦ Aids for Aides

EVERYONE needs ways of reaching children and giving them specific help. Good outreach programs provide initial training and give their participants tips for conducting sessions with the students, but a tutor or aide always needs a warehouse of ideas for future activities. That's the need the following descriptions are designed to fill—first for preschool, then for elementary-school age groups.

EARLY CHILDHOOD PROJECT
New York City

Dr. Martin Deutsch
Institute for Developmental Studies
School of Education
New York University
New York, New York

A. The Letter Form-Board for prekindergarten and kindergarten children was developed at the institute to provide a visual-motor experience in the development of letter-discrimination skills. It consisted of large wooden letters which were fitted into appropriately shaped slots on a board. The use of this board was based upon several assumptions: (1) the advantaged child may have facility with learning to read by whole-word methods because he is already familiar with the alphabet prior to first grade, but the disadvantaged child is not; (2) the board provides immediate answers to aid learning—the child knows that this response is correct only when the letter fits; (3) the process of making fine discriminations, such as between "O" and "Q," is learned; (4) the subsequent learning of the names and sounds will be easier if the children are first familiar with the letters on a purely visual and tactile basis.

Research with the board showed that untutored children did not profit greatly from working in pairs with more knowledgeable children (and presumably, then, should work alone or with others of their level). Another study revealed that children introduced to a few new letters each day learned much faster than those faced with all twenty-six letters from the first day.

B. Another technique used in the prekindergarten and kindergarten classes for the development of language was the game Language Lotto, which differs from standard lotto games in that it can be played at different language and conceptual levels, or using no language. Standard lotto games are usually restricted to nonverbal visual matching of pictures.

Language Lotto consists of six games, each with several boards and up to forty-eight cards. The games are ordered to proceed from simple to complex, from single words to sentences, from concrete to abstract. Familiar objects are pictured in the first game, prepositions in the second, actions in the third, and so forth. In each, the child learns first on a receptive level and then on a productive language level.

C. Matrix games were played by the preschoolers.
Ideally, what you should see is five or six children sitting in
small chairs in front of a board displaying sixteen pictures in
a 4-picture x 4-picture square. Examination of the pictures
reveals certain regularities: in the first column, all of the
children are holding cookies; in the second, all of the children are wearing gloves; in the third, all are drinking milk;
and in the fourth, all are wearing hats. Scanning the pictures
by rows reveals that each row has a common element: one
boy, two boys, one girl, and two girls.

If the children had been playing the games for a few
weeks, one of the children might be sitting in the adult chair
while the other four and the teacher are sitting in children's
chairs. The child playing the role of the teacher might be
heard saying to "her" class, "Close your eyes, no peeking."
Then she would get out of her chair and cover one of the
pictures with an opaque magnetized rectangle. "Now open
your eyes. Who can tell me something about the picture
that I covered?" Whereupon several of the children raise
their hands, and the child-teacher calls on one of them.

What is the content involved in figuring out the covered
picture? What must the child be able to do in order to come
up with the answer? To produce a complete answer, the
child must be able to (1) scan the pictures both vertically
and horizontally, (2) abstract the common element of both
the row and the column of the hidden picture, (3) combine
these two pieces of information, (4) produce the information
in a sentence, and (5) explain in words how he figured it out.
Underlying the solution to this type of matrix problem are
classificatory skills, which have been found to be more difficult for children from lower-class backgrounds than for their
middle-class peers, especially when the contents are presented by pictorial representation.

The Matrix Games curriculum has concerns other than

the complex abilities involved in solving the above problem. Within the context of the children's play there are other objectives: to speak clearly; to follow complex directions; to develop new vocabulary and concepts; and most important, to be an independent learner.

D. It has been frequently noted that disadvantaged children have a present-time orientation, with limited concepts of past, future, and extended time units such as weeks and months. A calendar curriculum was devised utilizing the principles of programmed instruction to teach these concepts. Each week the kindergarten teacher placed a one-week calendar of seven rectangles in a row upon the board. Saturday and Sunday, both together at the left, were marked with X's in colored chalk. Each day she placed an X in the box for that day. These X's were white, to distinguish school days from non-school days. She also mentioned the name of the day, but did not require yet that it be learned. As a second, third, or fourth row was added, the concept of *week* was learned and that of *month* began to be learned. The children also began to mark their own personal calendars each day. Teachers began to add variations, such as games which built number and phonic skills as well as names of days ("Find the box for the day in the third week that begins with the sound *t*").

E. A number of reading games were developed by the institute staff. These dealt mostly with first- and second-grade reading skills, and were played by two to four children. The following is an example:

SIGHT WORD BINGO

Purpose: The game offers practice in recognition of sight words taught in *Book B* of the Stern workbooks.

Materials: The game includes four playing boards,

each divided into twenty-five squares in which twenty-four sight words are printed, the same words in different squares on each board. The center square is a blank. Twenty-four sight word-cards and bingo chips are also included.

Play: The game can be played by two to four children. Each child takes one (or two) playing boards. All the players cover with a chip the blank space in the center of their boards. The word-cards are mixed and placed face down on the table. The first player picks the top word-card and reads the word. All the players then scan their boards, left to right, top row to bottom row. When a player finds the word on his board, he covers it with a chip.

After a word is read from a word-card, the card is placed face down on the table.

The child to the right of the first player picks the next word-card and reads the word. All the players again scan their boards and cover the word with a chip. The game continues in this fashion with players taking turns reading the word-cards. The first player to cover five words in any direction is the winner.

Preceding Activities: Children should be introduced to the sight word in *Book B* of the Stern workbooks before playing the game.

Succeeding Activities: Children should be introduced to additional sight words needed for reading specific easy reading books assigned by the teacher to the individual child. Children can make their own dictionaries for new sight words.

F. In the creative-dramatics activities, the teacher played any of several kinds of roles. For instance, when children had initiated a spontaneous play, she may have

entered as one of the characters who: (1) sought help
("Where do I buy my ticket for this train?"), (2) changed
the situation ("A child has just been hurt on the street. Can
you help us?"), or (3) added another dimension to the story
which the children had set up ("I have a lot of wonderful
gadgets for sale that you could use in your housework. May
I show them to you?").

Or, she may have assumed the usual teacher role in a
more direct initiation of dramatic play ("Let's pretend that
this rug is a boat. Where shall we go? Who will help row
the boat? Who will be the lookout?").

ACTIVITIES FOR AIDES

The following is a list of sample practices and procedures
which involved teacher aides in the Oakland, California, program. It must be stressed that an aide (or a volunteer) can
serve in a great variety of ways both in the classroom and on
the playground.

Manipulative Activity. Read to child; encourage child to
retell story using puppets; give suggestions for using materials such as pegs and mosaics to color or match designs;
name letters child uses in "fit-a-space"; help blindfold child
for matching-textures-and-shapes activity; help child with
sorting, categorizing, and sequence games; take attendance.

Language Development. Sit with children for group
lesson; participate with children and encourage those who
need it; lead finger plays or songs as teacher suggests; lead
small-group discussions on weather, calendar, and classroom
pets; prepare snack with child helper.

Snack. Sit with assigned group; encourage good man-
ners; encourage children to pass food and pour milk; encourage conversation; start one, if necessary, by using

picture or object; relate clean-up to classroom standards and individual responsibilities; develop concepts such as color, number, size.

Story Groups. Read story to groups; encourage children to discuss pictures and talk about story; let children suggest books to read.

Physical Development. Take out equipment for physical development; join children in ball and jump-rope play and organize games; encourage children to verbalize what they are doing; encourage children to play creatively on equipment; encourage developmental use of materials such as balancing, chinning, and climbing.

Creative Arts. Make a variety of materials available; encourage children to talk about art experiences (do not make suggestions); encourage correct use of materials and supervise clean-up; participate in walks, science experiences, or library visits; assist in preparation for going home—notes, children's work, and so on.

LANGUAGE STIMULATION PROGRAM
Auburn, Alabama

John L. Carter, Ph.D.
College of Education
University of Houston
Houston, Texas 77004

The stated objectives of this program were "to determine to what extent a systematic language development program will augment mental age and language scores of black educationally disadvantaged first-grade children" (Carter, 1967). It was assumed that the program would enhance test scores in language, mental age, and reading ability.

The Peabody language-learning materials and supplementary stories were used to stimulate the children's language development. To this end activities emphasized story-making, classifying, following directions, looking, counting, describing, and remembering. Examples follow.

Story-Making. The teacher presents a "space-scene" picture to the group and asks the children to make up a story about the picture. The teacher makes a tape recording of the story and plays it back for the class. Different children tell different stories as time permits.

Classifying. Five chairs are placed at the front of the room. A people card is placed on each chair. (People cards might include pictures of a mother, father, boy, girl, and baby.) Clothing cards are distributed among the children. Children come up one at a time and place their cards on the correct chair; for example, if a card shows clothing a baby would wear, the child places the card on the chair with the baby card.

Following Directions. The teacher gives oral directions for the group to follow in unison. For example: stand up, touch your hair, touch your shoulder, sit down. Or, in later lessons, directions might include: touch your nose with your left hand, put your right hand on your left ear, put your left hand on your right shoulder.

Looking. The children are asked to look around the room very carefully. The teacher asks them to name as many things (objects) as they can. Each child is asked to name one object and to tell what it is used for.

Counting. The teacher presents number cards and asks the group to name them (numbers) in unison. The children are guided to name the cards first in sequence and then in random order. Each pupil is asked to count to ten.

Describing. Describing activities frequently serve multiple goals. For example, in one such activity, color cards are placed on the chalk tray (red, orange, yellow, green, and blue). Picking up one card, the teacher asks children whose

clothes are the color of the card to stand up. Each child who
stands up tells the others what he is wearing of that color.
The teacher asks some pupils to give a complete description
of their clothing. This particular activity gives children practice in naming and classifying (colors) in addition to developing complete sentences for their oral descriptions.

Remembering. The teacher reads a simple poem to the
children. She repeats the poem, letting the children complete
the last word in each line. The teacher asks the children to
recall some information emphasized in the poem. After
prompting the group by reading the first half of a line from
the poem, the teacher asks individual children and, finally, the
group in unison to complete the line correctly. (A regular
remembering activity was developed around the supplementary story read by the teacher at the end of each lesson.
Not only would children answer questions about the
story immediately after hearing it read, but also they would
be asked questions about the story the following day.)

Listening. Of course, listening was integral to all of the
activities illustrated above. However, specific training in
listening skills may be illustrated by the following activity:
the teacher reads word lists, having told the children to clap
their hands when they hear the name of a number (dive—
five—hive—ton—*ten*).

The tape recorder was used almost daily. A typical
lesson (about fifty minutes) might begin with a tape re-
corded story of, say, *Goldilocks and the Three Bears.* The
children would be asked to recall the names of the characters.
The teacher would retell the story, stopping after the word
"said," to let individual children take the parts of the story's
characters and finish their sentences. The next activity might
involve classifying and naming pictures on cards, perhaps
making up a story about some of the pictures or describing
characteristics of the pictured objects. The third activity in

the day's lesson might be a counting game in which a few of
the children are given one number card each. As the teacher
calls out a number, the child holding that number stands up,
says his number out loud, and calls another number. If the
child fails to stand up when his number is called, he loses
his card to a child who does not have one, and the game continues. The fourth activity in the day's lesson might be a
following-directions game, followed by the final daily activity, "Story Time." The daily story was usually preceded
by questions about the previous day's story and followed by
questions on the story just read.

As indicated earlier, the ten-week Language Stimulation Program covered the first forty lessons in the Peabody
Language Development Kit. A daily lesson, such as described
above, would cover one of these Peabody lessons and additional activities pulled from Peabody lessons 41-280, and the
supplementary story which the teacher selected from a
variety of sources. These stories might be fairy tales (*Sleeping
Beauty*) or stories from other cultures (*Blaze and the Indian
Cave*), or stories about careers (*I Want to Be a Teacher*),
and so on.

LEARNING TO LEARN PROGRAM
Jacksonville, Florida

Dr. Herbert A. Sprigle
Learning to Learn School, Inc.
1936 San Marco Boulevard
Jacksonville, Florida 32207

General Methods. The Learning to Learn Program was
organized around certain basic principles of mental growth
and child development. One assumption was that development of the child's ability to think, reason, and learn follows
an orderly sequence of growth with periods of transition.

Based on past child-development research, it was further
assumed that this sequence proceeds from motor to perceptual
to symbolic levels. Additional principles of mental growth
and child development which were basic to the program
may be paraphrased as follows:

Learning is an active, continuing process that occurs
when material the child uses possesses certain properties: (1)
it must be appealing and attractive enough to arouse the
child's curiosity; (2) it must make the child feel reasonably
sure of what he is doing; and (3) it must direct the child
to a goal and at the same time give him some idea of where
he is with respect to the goal.

The methods employed to teach the young child must
be flexible, play-oriented, and adaptable to different developmental and learning levels (Sprigle, in Van De Riet & Van De
Riet, Appendix A, 1966).

The Learning to Learn curriculum, materials, classroom
physical arrangements, and orientation of teachers were
structured on all of these theories. The material is available
from Science Research Associates: *Inquisitive Games, Discovering How to Learn* and *Inquisitive Games, Exploring
Number and Space,* by H. A. Sprigle.

Specific Methods. The language-oriented games and related activities were designed to develop the child's abilities
to perceive, recognize, categorize, and discover relationships.
Games and activities were arranged in sequence to develop
and gradually extend the child's ability to talk about and
deal with things and ideas in the abstract, or in the absence
of any tangible objects or relationships. Language became a
tool for thinking, reasoning, and communicating things that
the child had not said or heard before. The games went beyond the teaching of language and communication skills.
The child also was given opportunities for the development
of strategies of gathering information, problem-solving, and
decision-making.

SELF-DIRECTIVE DRAMATIZATION PROJECT
Joliet, Illinois

Dr. Leslie Carlton
Department of Education
Illinois State University
Normal, Illinois

Reading ability is obviously basic to learning all other
subjects and at all stages of the educational process. Therefore the claim that Carlton and Moore set out to test, starting
with culturally disadvantaged children, entailed concepts
such as: Self-directive dramatization—therapy for emotional
problems—reading practice—improvement in self-concept
and reading ability—increase in desire to achieve, and for
higher goals—new leverage in other directions—greater
successes.

A brief glossary may be helpful.

Self-directive. The positive aspect of "nondirective";
the teacher maintains an unobtrusive presence but encourages
the pupil to make his own decisions and choices—within
the framework.

Dramatization. Not play-reading, nor amateur theatri-
cals. "Self-directive dramatization of stories . . . is the
pupil's own original, imaginative, spontaneous interpretation
of a character of his own choosing in a story which he has
selected and read cooperatively with other pupils in his group
which was formed for the time being and for a particular
story only." (Carlton and Moore, 1968, p. 10.)

Self-Concept. "Involves what an individual thinks he is,
what he thinks he can do, what he thinks he cannot do."
(Carlton and Moore, 1968, p. 11.)

The only special materials used consisted of about two
hundred books which contained stories suitable for each
grade level, there being a few score books for each level. Al-

though for a start these were fiction, there were also factual, biographical, and historical books.

To get children started, the teacher selected about five stories for a class of twenty-five to thirty pupils of varying reading levels; she listed these and the characters involved on the board in order to demonstrate the procedure to be followed without her help thereafter. Each pupil then selected the story he wished to read with others in the group; the number of characters involved determined the size of the group. There would be five or six such groups who then gathered in different parts of the room, and pupils took turns at reading parts of stories aloud until the story had been read. Each pupil then selected the character he wished to portray when the story was dramatized. Conflicts in choices were resolved by the children themselves. Groups then took turns in dramatizing the story for the rest of the class. No rehearsals, costumes, or props were used, and a different leader was chosen in each group for each story. This leader helped in organization and prompting, and he called for help from the teacher in pronunciation, or for any other problems which the children could not solve for themselves. On all occasions after the first, children went through the whole process of selecting stories, grouping themselves, selecting characters, choosing a leader, resolving conflicts, etc., with minimal assistance from the teacher. However, when a child had requested it and called attention to the need, children were given opportunities to read to the teacher, who did remedial work where necessary.

Examples of stories and books used are:

Grade 1: *Merry-Go-Round*, "The Little Red Hen," Charles E. Merrill Publishing Co.; *Up and Away*, "Pails and Pails of Paint," Houghton Mifflin Company.

Grade 2: *Friends and Neighbors*, "City Mouse and Country Mouse," Scott, Foresman and Co.; *Come Along,*

"Traffic Policeman," Houghton Mifflin Company.

Grade 7: *Parades*, "The Story of Penicillin," Scott, Foresman and Co.; *High Trails*, "Mama and the Graduation Present," Allyn and Bacon, Inc.

SCHOOL AND HOME PROGRAM
Flint, Michigan

Dr. Mildred B. Smith
Area Director of Elementary Education
Administration Building
Flint Public Schools
Flint, Michigan

A. *Read-Aloud Program.* Parents were encouraged to read with their children in order to stimulate interest in reading and to show the children that reading is important to parents. This not only improved reading performance but also encouraged parent-child interactions conducive to a more desirable family relationship. The Read-Aloud Program consisted of orientation of the parents at the introductory meeting with teachers, and instructions on a sheet and in a booklet. A three-by-five card imprinted with the title of each study step was also included in these materials as a study-instruction aid. The instruction sheet for the parent looked like this (Flint, 1963):

HOW PARENTS CAN HELP THEIR CHILDREN STUDY
READING WORDS

Children benefit from studying with another person as well as from individual study. This other person may be a classmate, an older child, or a parent.

It is very encouraging to children to have a parent spend some time with him while he is studying. *We must always keep in mind that it is the child who must do the studying, not the parent. The parent only assists and gives encouragement.*

When you help your child study his reading words, we suggest that you and the child follow the study steps. Listed below are these study steps as well as suggestions about what the child should do and what the parent should do.

The child should:	*Study Steps*
1. LOOK AT THE WORD	Look at only one word at a time. Think about its shape and how it begins and ends.
2. SAY THE WORD	Say it softly. Think about how it sounds.
3. TELL WHAT IT MEANS	The meaning should be in *your own words.*
4. TRY TO USE IT IN A SENTENCE	Your sentence should be a good sentence. It should make sense.
5. CHECK THE WORD	Check to see that you have given the correct meaning and used it in a sentence. If you made a mistake, start with Step 1 and go through the steps again.

The parent should:

1. Sit close to the child so that you can see what the child is doing.
2. See that the child pronounces the word correctly.
3. Help the child check his word so that he does not learn the wrong meaning for it. If this happens, en-

courage him to go through the study steps again
until he:

a. can say it correctly
b. can say the meaning in his own words
c. can use it in a sentence

*Remember that you always can help your child
more when you are patient and not hurried.*

In addition to the above instructions, a booklet entitled
"Read Aloud to Your Children" was given to the parents. In
this booklet, the how, when, and what of reading as well
as the motivational techniques for both parent and child
were presented. To stimulate reading of new books, lists of
books for various grade levels available at the local Flint
Public Libraries were included.

B. *Bookworm Club.* A reading incentive program called
the Bookworm Club was initiated in this program. Children
in grades two through six were given a tally sheet on which
they placed stickers provided for the fifteen segments of a
"bookworm"—one for each new book read. This program
allowed each child to earn a "bookworm" lapel button
when six segments were covered, and a "diploma" when
all fifteen were covered. Children were also given a booklet
called "My Reading Record" in which they would write
the author, title, publisher, date, and a summary of each book
they read.

C. *Reading Booklets.* Reading booklets for the children
were made by cutting up primary-level reading textbooks
which were no longer used by the schools. Individual stories
from these books were stapled together between colorful
covers and decorated with pictures.

Children who have trouble reading resist thick books
because they lack confidence in their reading abilities. These
children will readily read the one-story booklets which have

no grade-level identification. Older children will read these stories, not aware that many of the stories contain pre-primer-level vocabulary. The children develop a feeling of accomplishment and, therefore, gain self-confidence.

Mothers did the cutting and stapling of the one-story booklets and felt a sense of participation in their children's reading program. The children were aware of their mothers' participation, and this stimulated additional interest and interaction on the part of children and parents.

.

Bibliography

THE SUCCESS of any volunteer program in education depends on the wisdom and sensitivity of its tutors; therefore, the orientation and training of tutors is very important. As a starter, most programs suggest tutors read popular books on education, such as *Teacher* by Sylvia Ashton-Warner or *Up the Down Staircase* by Bel Kaufman. Then the tutor may be led into the deeper waters of child development and educational psychology. He or she may need to acquire special skills in his tutoring area and become familiar with professional materials. In addition, the programs for disadvantaged children require an awareness of urban problems that are described from many points of view in today's literature. Handbooks from well-established volunteer programs in the larger cities include their own lists of recommended reading. Because individual programs may be filling a particular need and may have a specific focus, the following books selected from across the nation are presented in these categories:

1. Education in general
2. Specific help in the area of reading
3. Books for children and young adults
4. Urban problems, ethnic books and bibliographies

READING LISTS FOR VOLUNTEERS

EDUCATION IN GENERAL

Ashton-Warner, Sylvia. *Teacher*. New York: Simon and Schuster, 1963.

Broudy, Harry S. *The Real World of Public Schools*. New York: Harcourt Brace Jovanovich, 1972.

Bruner, J. S. *The Process of Education*. New York: Random House, 1960.

Carter, Barbara, and Dapper, Gloria. *School Volunteers: What They Do. How They Do It*. New York: Citation Press, 1972.

Dennison, George. *The Lives of Children*. New York: Random House, 1969.

Dinkmeyer, Don, and Dreikurs, R. *Encouraging Children to Learn*. Englewood Cliffs, N.J.: Prentice-Hall, 1963.

Fass, Jerome S. *Primer for Parents*. Boston: Houghton Mifflin Co., 1966.

Fraiberg, Selma. *The Magic Years*. New York: Charles Scribner's Sons, 1968.

Frymier, Jack R. *The Nature of the Educational Method*. Columbus, Ohio: Charles E. Merrill Publishing Co., 1965.

Graubard, Allen. *Free the Children: Radical Reform and the Free-School Movement*. New York: Pantheon Books, 1973.

Holt, John. *How Children Fail*. New York: Dell Publishing Co., 1970.

————. *How Children Learn*. New York: Dell Publishing Co., 1970.

Hymes, James L., Jr. *A Child Development Point of View*. Englewood Cliffs, N.J.: Prentice-Hall, 1955.

Janowitz, Gayle. *Helping Hands: Volunteer Work in Education*. Chicago: University of Chicago Press, 1966.

Jencks, Christopher, et al. *Inequality: A Reassessment of the Effect of Family and Schooling in America*. New York: Basic Books, 1972.

Kaufman, Bel. *Up the Down Staircase*. Englewood Cliffs, N.J.: Prentice-Hall, 1964.

Mearns and Hughes, eds. *Creative Power: The Education of Youth in the Creative Arts*. New York: Dover Publications, 1958.

O'Gorman, Ned. *The Wilderness and the Laurel Tree: A Guide for Teachers and Parents on the Observation of Children*. New York: Harper and Row, 1972.

Pepe, Thomas J. *Free and Inexpensive Educational Aids*. New York: Dover Publications, 1962.

Redl, Fritz, and Wineman, David. *The Aggressive Child*. New York: The Free Press, 1957.

————. *Children Who Hate*. New York: The Free Press, 1951.

————. *Controls from Within*. New York: The Free Press, 1952.

Rosenthal, Robert, and Jacobson, Lenore. *Pygmalion in the Classroom: Teacher Expectation and Pupil's Intellectual Ability*. New York: Holt, Rinehart and Winston, 1968.

Russell, James E. *Change and Challenge in American Education*. Boston: Houghton Mifflin Co., 1965.

Schrag, Peter. *Village School Downtown*. Boston: Beacon Press, 1967.

Silberman, Charles. *Crisis in the Classroom*. New York: Random House, 1970.

Smith, A. G., ed. *Communication and Culture: Readings in the Codes of Human Interaction*. New York: Holt, Rinehart and Winston, 1966.

IN THE AREA OF READING

I. The following handbooks were written specifically for tutoring programs in reading:

Keene, Teresa, comp. *Tips for Tutors: A Manual for Reading Improvement*. Chicago: Chicago Public Library, 1970.

Laffey, James, and Perkins, Phyllis. *Teacher Orientation Handbook*. Washington, D.C.: National Reading Center, 1972.

Lundblad, Helen, and Smith, Carl B. *Tutor Trainers Handbook*. Washington, D.C.: National Reading Center, 1972.

Mergentime, Charlotte. *School Volunteer Reading Reference Handbook*. New York: School Volunteer Program, 20 West Fortieth Street, 1965.

Project VOICE (Voluntary Opportunities for Inspiring Coordinators of Education). *A Coordinator's "How to Do" Handbook*. Washington, D.C.: Volunteers in Education, U.S. Office of Education, 1971.

Rauch, Sidney J., ed. *Handbook for the Volunteer Tutor*. Newark, Del.: International Reading Association, 1969.

Robbins, Edward L. *Tutors Handbook*. Washington, D.C.: National Reading Center, 1972.

Swanson, Mary T. *Your Volunteer Program: Organization and Administration of Volunteer Programs*. Ankeny, Iowa: Des Moines Area Community College, 1970.

Tampa Model Cities Program. *Tutoring Manual: Intensive Tutorial*. Tampa, Fla., 1970.

Tuinman, J. Jaap. *Approaches to the Teaching of Reading*. Washington, D.C.: National Reading Center, 1972.

U.S. Department of Health, Education and Welfare, Office of Citizen Participation. *Volunteers in Education: Materials for Volunteer Programs and the Volunteer*. Washington, D.C., 1970.

Wilson Library Bulletin, Vol. 45, no. 3 (November, 1970). This issue was devoted to the librarian and the teaching of reading.

II. Other important books for reading tutors are:

Botel, Morton, et al. *How to Teach Reading*. Chicago: Follett Publishing Co., 1963.

Chall, Jeanne. *Learning to Read: The Great Debate*. New York: McGraw-Hill Book Co., 1967.

Cleary, Florence Damon. *Blueprints for Better Reading: School Programs for Promoting Skill and Interest in Reading*. New York: The H. W. Wilson Co., 1972.

Cohen, S. Allen. *Teach Them All to Read: Methods and Materials for Teaching the Disadvantaged*. New York: Random House, 1969.

Conroy, Sophie. *Specifics for You: A Corrective Reading Handbook*. Brooklyn, N.Y.: Book-Lab, 1966.

Dietrich, Dorothy M., and Mathews, Virginia H., eds. *Reading and Revolution: The Role of Reading in Today's Society*. Newark, Del.: International Reading Association, 1970.

Gans, Roma. *Common Sense in Teaching Reading*. Indianapolis: The Bobbs-Merrill Co., 1963.

Gray, Lillian. *Teaching Children to Read*. New York: The Ronald Press Co., 1963.

Harris, Albert J. *Effective Teaching of Reading*. New York: David McKay Co., 1962.

———. *How to Increase Reading Ability*. New York: David McKay Co., 1961.

Jennison, Peter S., and Sheridan, Robert N., eds. *The Future of General Adult Books and Reading in America.* Chicago: American Library Association, 1970.

Karlin, Robert, ed. *Teaching Reading in High School: Selected Articles.* Indianapolis: The Bobbs-Merrill Co., 1969.

Kottmeyer, William. *Teacher's Guide for Remedial Reading.* New York: McGraw-Hill Book Co., 1958.

Lee, Dorris M., and Allen, Richard V. *Learning to Read Through Experience.* New York: Appleton-Century-Crofts, 1963.

Love, Harold D. *Parents Diagnose and Correct Reading Problems.* Springfield, Ill.: Charles C. Thomas, 1970.

McCullough, C. M. *Teaching Elementary Reading.* New York: Appleton-Century-Crofts, 1968.

Mergentime, Charlotte. *You and Your Child's Reading.* New York: Harcourt Brace Jovanovich, 1963.

National School Public Relations Association. *Reading Crisis: The Problem and Suggested Solutions: An Education USA Special Report.* Washington, D.C., 1970.

Otto, Wayne, and Ford, David. *Teaching Adults to Read.* Boston: Houghton Mifflin Co., 1967.

Pope, Lillie. *Guidelines to Teaching Remedial Reading to the Disadvantaged.* Brooklyn, N.Y.: Book-Lab, 1969.

Robinson, H. Alan, ed. *The Underachiever in Reading: Conference on Reading.* Chicago: University of Chicago Press, 1962.

Russell, David, and Karp, Etta. *Reading Aids Through the Grades.* New York: Teachers College Press, 1951.

Scott, Louise Band, and Thompson, Jesse J. *Talking Time.* New York: McGraw-Hill Book Co., 1966.

Sleisenger, Lenore. *Guidebook for the Volunteer Reading Teacher.* New York: Teachers College Press, 1965.

Smith, Carl B., ed. *Parents and Reading.* Newark, Del.: International Reading Association, 1971.

Smith, Edwin H. and Marie P. *Teaching Reading to Adults.* Washington, D.C.: National Association for Public School Adult Educators, 1962.

Strang, Ruth, et al. *The Improvement of Reading.* New York: McGraw-Hill Book Co., 1967.

Wuebker, Virginia B. *You, Your Child and Reading.* New York: Pageant Press International Corp., 1970.

Zintz, Miles V. *The Reading Process: The Teacher and the Learner.* Dubuque, Iowa: William C. Brown Co., 1970.

BOOKS FOR CHILDREN AND YOUNG ADULTS

Here are some guides to the wonderful world of children's books. They will remind parents of the old favorites and introduce them to the best of the new books.

American Library Association. *Let's Read Together: Books for Family Enjoyment.* Chicago, 1969.

Arbuthnot, May. *Children and Books.* Glenview, Ill.: Scott, Foresman and Co., 1964.

———, et al. *Children's Books Too Good to Miss.* Cleveland: Case-Western Reserve University Press, 1964.

Carlsen, G. Robert. *Books and the Teen-Age Reader: A Guide for Teachers, Librarians and Parents,* 2d ed. New York: Harper and Row and Bantam Books, 1971.

Causley, Charles, ed. *Modern Ballads and Story Poems.* New York: Franklin Watts, 1965.

Dunning, Stephen; Lueders, Edward; and Smith, Hugh, eds. *Reflections on a Gift of Watermelon Pickle and Other Modern Verse.* Glenview, Ill.: Scott, Foresman and Co., 1966.

Eaton, Anne T. *Reading with Children.* New York: The Viking Press, 1940.

Fraiberg, Selma. *The Magic Years.* New York: Charles Scribner's Sons, 1968.

Frank, Josette. *Your Child's Reading Today.* 3d ed. New York: Doubleday and Co., 1969.

Hazard, Paul. *Books, Children and Men.* Boston: Horn Book, 1960.

Johnson, Edna, et al., eds. *Anthology of Children's Literature.* Boston: Houghton Mifflin Co., 1970.

Larrick, Nancy. *A Parent's Guide to Children's Reading.* 3d ed. New York: Doubleday and Co. and Pocket Books, 1969.

Livingston, Myra Cohn, ed. *A Tune Beyond Us: A Collection of Poetry.* New York: Harcourt Brace Jovanovich, 1968.

Mergentime, Charlotte. *You and Your Child's Reading.* New York: Harcourt Brace Jovanovich, 1967.

Mott, Carolyn, and Baisden, Leo B. *Children's Book on How to Use Books and Libraries.* New York: Charles Scribner's Sons, 1964.

Painter, Helen W., ed. *Reaching Children and Young People*

Through Literature. Newark, Del.: International Reading Association, 1971.

Pilgrim, Geneva H., and McAllister, Mariana K. *Books, Young People and Reading Guidance.* 2d ed. New York: Harper and Row, 1968.

Sawyer, Ruth. *The Way of the Storyteller.* New York: The Viking Press, 1965.

Shedlock, Marie. *The Art of the Story-teller.* New York: Dover Publications, 1951.

Smith, Dora V. *Fifty Years of Children's Books.* Champaign, Ill.: National Council of Teachers of English, 1963.

Smith, Lillian H. *Unreluctant Years.* New York: The Viking Press, 1967.

Smith, James S. *A Critical Approach to Children's Literature.* New York: McGraw-Hill Book Co., 1967.

Walsh, Frances, ed. *That Eager Zest: First Discoveries in the Magic World of Books.* Philadelphia: J. B. Lippincott Co., 1961.

URBAN PROBLEMS AND ETHNIC BOOKS

The School Volunteer Program in New York City suggests the following books as background material for its trainees:

Ashton-Warner, Sylvia. *Teacher.* New York: Simon and Schuster, 1963.

Coles, Robert. *Children of Crisis.* New York: Dell Publishing Co., 1968.

Dennison, George. *The Lives of Children.* New York: Random House, 1969.

Fader, Daniel N., and McNeill, Elton. *Hooked on Books: Program and Proof.* New York: Berkley Publishing Corp., 1968.

Glazer, Nathan and Moynihan, Daniel. *Beyond the Melting Pot.* Cambridge, Mass.: The M.I.T. Press, 1964.

Griffin, John H. *Black Like Me.* New York: The New American Library, 1961.

Hentoff, Nat. *Our Children Are Dying.* New York: The Viking Press, 1966.

Herndon, James. *The Way It Spozed to Be.* New York: Simon and Schuster, 1968.

Kozol, Jonathan. *Death at an Early Age*. Boston: Houghton Mifflin Co., 1967.

Lewis, Oscar. *La Vida: A Puerto Rican Family in the Culture of Poverty, San Juan and New York*. New York: Random House, 1966.

Riessman, Frank. *The Culturally Deprived Child*. New York: Harper and Row, 1962.

Other books about urban problems and teaching disadvantaged children are:

Book, John W., and Saxe, Richard. *Teaching the Culturally Disadvantaged Pupil*. Springfield, Ill.: Charles C. Thomas, 1969.

Bereiter, Carl, and Engelmann, S. *Language and Learning Difficulties for the Disadvantaged Child*. New York: Anti-Defamation League of B'nai B'rith.

Cheney, Arnold B., ed. *The Ripe Harvest: Educating Migrant Children*. Miami: University of Miami Press, 1972.

Clark, Kenneth B. *Dark Ghetto*. New York: Harper and Row, 1965.

———, and Jeannette Hopkins. *Relevant War Against Poverty: A Study of Community Action Programs and Observable Social Change*. New York: Harper and Row, 1969.

Fader, Daniel. *The Naked Children*. New York: The Macmillan Co., 1971.

Harrington, Michael. *The Other America*. New York: The Macmillan Co., 1962.

Howard, John R., ed. *Awakening Minorities: American Indians, Mexican Americans and Puerto Ricans*. Chicago: Aldine-Atherton, 1970.

Kozol, Jonathan. *Free Schools*. New York: Bantam Books, 1972.

Lewis, Oscar. *A Study of Slum Culture: Backgrounds of La Vida*. New York: Random House, 1968.

Riessman, Frank. *Helping the Disadvantaged Pupil to Learn More Easily*. Englewood Cliffs, N.J.: Prentice-Hall, 1966.

Rosen, Carl L., and Ortego, Philip D. *Issues in Language and Reading Instruction of Spanish-speaking Children: An Annotated Bibliography*. Newark, Del.: International Reading Association, 1969.

Sexton, Patricia. *Education and Income*. New York: The Viking Press, 1961.

Silberman, Charles E. *Crisis in Black and White*. New York: Random House, 1964.

Steiner, Stan. *La Raza*. New York: Harper and Row, 1969.

Taba, Hilda, and Elkins, Deborah. *Teaching Strategies for the Culturally Disadvantaged*. Chicago: Rand McNally and Co., 1966.

Thomas, Piri. *Down These Mean Streets*, New York: Alfred A. Knopf and The New American Library, 1967.

Webster, Staten W. *The Disadvantaged Learner*. San Francisco: Chandler Publishing Co., 1966.

Weinberg, Meyer. *The Education of the Minority Child: A Comprehensive Bibliography of 10,000 Selected Entries*. Chicago: Integrated Education Associates, 1970.

Zeonin, Joseph M. *The Control of Urban Schools: Perspective on the Power of Educational Reform*. New York: The Free Press, 1973.

The following are anthologies and bibliographic resources concerning ethnic groups:

Alegria, Ricardo E. *Three Wishes: A Collection of Puerto Rican Folktales*. New York: Harcourt Brace Jovanovich, 1969.

Antell, Will and Lee, comp. *American Indians: An Annotated Bibliography of Selected Library Resources*. Minneapolis: Minnesota State Department of Education, Minnesota University, College of Education, 1970.

Baker, Augusta. *The Black Experience in Children's Books*. New York: New York Public Library, Office of Children's Services, 1971.

Barrios, Ernie, ed. *Bibliografía de Aztlan: An Annotated Chicano Bibliography*. San Diego, Calif.: Centro de Estudios Chicanos Pub., 5716 Lindo Paseo, 1971.

Baxter, Katherine, comp. *The Black Experience and the School Curriculum: Teaching Materials for Grades K-12: An Annotated Bibliography*. Philadelphia: Wellsprings Ecumenical Center, 6380 Germantown Avenue, 1968.

Belpre, Pura. *The Tiger and the Rabbit and Other Tales*. Philadelphia: J. B. Lippincott Co., 1965.

Brandon, William. *The Magic World*. New York: William Morrow and Co., 1971. American Indian Songs and Poetry.

Cain, Alfred E. *Negro Heritage Reader for Young People.* Yonkers, N.Y.: Education Heritage, Inc., 1965.

Clarke, J. Henrick, ed. *American Negro Short Stories.* New York: Holt, Rinehart and Winston, 1966.

Conwell, Mary K., Pura, and Belpre. *Libros en Español: An Annotated List of Children's Books in Spanish.* New York: New York Public Library, Office of Children's Services, 1971.

Day, A. Grove. *The Sky Clears: Poetry of the American Indians.* Lincoln, Nebr.: University of Nebraska Press, 1964.

Dwyer, Carlotta Cardenas, comp. *Bibliography of Chicano Literature: For Children, Young People and Adults with a Section on Chicano Education.* Urbana, Ill., National Council of Teachers of English, 1972.

Emanuel, James A., and Gross, Theodore L. *Dark Symphony: Negro Literature in America.* New York: The Free Press, 1968.

Flores, Angel, ed. *Great Spanish Short Stories.* New York: Dell Publishing Co., 1956.

Hirschfelder, Arlene B., comp. *American Indian Authors: A Representative Bibliography.* New York: Association on American Indian Affairs, 1970.

————. *An Annotated Bibliography of Selected Children's Books about American Indians.* New York: Association on American Indian Affairs, 1972.

Jackson, Miles M., Jr., ed. *Bibliography of Negro History and Culture for Young Readers.* Pittsburgh: University of Pittsburgh Press, 1968.

James, Charles L. *From the Roots: Short Stories by Black Americans.* New York: Dodd, Mead and Co., 1970.

Jordan, June. *Soulscript.* New York: Doubleday and Co., 1970.

Lamb, Ruth S. *Mexican Americans: Sons of the Southwest.* Claremont, Calif.: Ocelot Press, 1970.

Lewis, Richard. *Out of the Earth I Sing: Poetry and Songs of Primitive Peoples of the World.* New York: W. W. Norton and Co., 1968.

Lomax, Alan, and Abdul, Raoul, eds. *3,000 Years of Black Poetry.* New York: Dodd, Mead and Co., 1970.

Ludwig, Edward, and Santibanez, James. *The Chicanos: Mexican American Voices.* Baltimore: Penguin Books, 1971.

Marriott, Alice, and Rachlin, Carol K. *American Indian Mythology.* New York: Thomas Y. Crowell, 1968.

Miller, Elizabeth W., comp. *The Negro in America: A Bibliography*. Cambridge, Mass.: Harvard University Press, 1966.

National Association for the Advancement of Colored People. *Integrated School Books: A Descriptive Bibliography of 399 Preschool and Elementary School Texts and Story Books*. New York, 1967.

New York Public Library, Office of Young Adult Services. *Black America: Books, Films, Recordings: A Selected List for Young Adults*. New York, 1970.

———, Office of Adult Services. *No Crystal Stair: A Bibliography of Black Literature*. New York, 1971.

Resnick, Seymour. *Spanish-American Poetry: A Bilingual Selection*. Irvington-on-Hudson, N.Y.: Harvey House, 1962.

Rollins, Charlemae. *We Build Together: A Bibliography*. Urbana, Ill.: National Council of Teachers of English, 1969.

Romano-V., Octavio I. *El Espejo/The Mirror: Selected Mexican American Literature*. Berkeley, California: Quinto Sol Publications, 1969.

Shular, Antonia Castaneda; Ybarra-Frausto, Tomas; Sommers, Joseph. *Literatura Chicana, Texto y Contexto: Chicano Literature, Text and Context*. Englewood Cliffs, N.J.: Prentice-Hall, 1972.

Spache, George. *Good Reading for the Disadvantaged: Multiethnic Resources*. Champaign, Ill.: Garrard Publishing Co., 1970.

Treworgy, Mildred L., and Foreman, Paul B. eds. *Negroes in the United States: A Bibliography of Materials for Schools*. University Park, Pa.: Pennsylvania State University Library, 1968.

Valdez, Luis, and Steiner, Stan. *Aztlan: An Anthology of Mexican American Literature*. New York: Random House, 1972.

Wolfe, Ann G., comp. *About 100 Books: A Gateway to Better Intergroup Understanding*. New York: Institute of Human Relations, American Jewish Committee, 1969.

Zirkel, Perry Alan, comp. *A Bibliography of Materials in English and Spanish Relating to Puerto Rican Students*. Hartford, Conn.: Connecticut Migratory Children's Program, University of Hartford, 1971.

NOTE

Reading is Fun-damental publishes an attractive "Guide to Book Selection" listing paperbacks and inexpensive books for elementary grades. Copies are available upon request from Room 2407, Arts and Industries Building, Smithsonian Institution, Washington, D.C. 20560. A valuable section of this booklet gives special book lists for ethnic groups—Black, Indian and Spanish-speaking—at the elementary level and for teenagers and adults.

Several libraries and projects included in this book have compiled lists for special purposes. The Reader Development Program of the Free Library of Philadelphia (236 North Twenty-third Street, Philadelphia, Pa. 19103) has an excellent annotated and graded bibliography for instructors, tutors, reading specialists, social workers and others working with the undereducated. A wide range of subjects is covered: leisure reading, the community, family life, jobs, reading, writing, arithmetic, science, the world and its people. The first bibliography appeared in January, 1971, with supplements in January, 1972, and June, 1972. Most large library systems regularly prepare lists of recommended books for special groups (ethnic minorities) and children and young people, and should also be contacted.